Beyond Jabez

BEYOND JABEZ

BRUCE WILKINSON

WITH BRIAN SMITH

Multnomah Books

BEYOND JABEZ
published by Multnomah Books

© 2005 by Exponential, Inc.
ISBN-13: 978-1-590-52671-2

Cover design by Brand Navigation, LLC
Cover image by Steve Gardner/PixelWorks Studio

Unless otherwise indicated, Scripture quotations are from:
The Holy Bible, New King James Version
© 1984 by Thomas Nelson, Inc.

Other Scripture quotations are from:
The Holy Bible, King James Version (KJV)

Published in the United States by WaterBrook Multnomah, an imprint of
the Crown Publishing Group, a division of Random House Inc., New York.

MULTNOMAH and its mountain colophon are registered trademarks
of Random House Inc.

For information:
MULTNOMAH BOOKS
12265 Oracle Boulevard, Suite 200
Colorado Springs, CO 80921

146673257

CONTENTS

ACKNOWLEDGMENTS

To all who—like those individuals in the book of Acts—look at who they are now and who they will never be, at what they can do and what they will never be able to do…and still dare to ask God for the world.

May you personally experience "the exceeding greatness of His power toward us" (Ephesians 1:19). You will find that He is more than able, and more than desirous, to "do exceedingly abundantly above all that we ask or think" (Ephesians 3:20).

Without the editorial skills of Brian Smith and David Webb, the marketing insights of Guy Coleman, and the encouragement of the Multnomah team and publisher Don Jacobson, *Beyond Jabez* would never have found its way to paper. Thank you, my friends, for your commitment to carefully stewarding this message.

THE LITTLE PRAYER
THAT COULD

*W*hen *The Prayer of Jabez* was first published in the spring of 2000, if you had told me that this little ninety-three-page book would become "the fastest-selling book of all time"—as *Publishers Weekly* dubbed it in 2002—I wouldn't have believed it. But the response has been, and continues to be, incredible. Even now, I employ a full-time assistant to answer e-mails and letters from people writing to tell me of their Jabez experiences! And the stories continue to flood in from those who have tasted the miracle of answered prayer.

Wherever I go, wherever I teach, the question is always the same: "How can you explain the sales of your book?" After a couple of years, I felt that the answer had become apparent; after all, nearly everywhere I went, someone rushed up to share their own story: "You should hear *what God did* when I prayed the prayer of Jabez…"

I remember speaking at the Billy Graham Cove where an

informal poll revealed that more than 80 percent of the audience had purchased multiple copies to give as gifts to their family and friends. One man had given away more than eighty cases! Why? He told me, "For some reason, God is answering this prayer in the life of everyone I have given it to—and I want everyone I know to experience the reality that God answers prayer!"

The phrase "You should hear what God did" may be the key to the unprecedented success of *The Prayer of Jabez.* Millions of people have told millions of others what God has done in their lives in answer to this simple prayer. And when one person tells another what God has done, that's giving God the credit He so richly deserves.

JABEZ IN AFRICA

I'm also convinced that the prayer of Jabez is directly linked to the call to launch a global movement called Dream for Africa. After the success of the book and its follow-up, *Secrets of the Vine,* our family unexpectedly felt called to move to Africa and help with efforts to stop the AIDS epidemic, perhaps the greatest crisis to hit mankind since the great Flood. When the call came, I inquired of the Lord, "Are you sure? After all, I'm not in my twenties anymore. Or my thirties. Or my forties."

I had to smile from the gentle nudge that came back: *But aren't you the Jabez guy? Haven't you been pleading with Me for decades for much, much more territory? Are we going to debate where the boundaries of that territory lie?*

During this season, I returned to Matthew 28:18–20 and meditated on the Great Commission for months, asking the

Lord to reveal to me if I had missed anything vital to the next chapter in my service for Him. I discovered in that study something very significant—something that I knew, yet didn't know—that would change my life forever.

Jesus commanded His followers to disciple all "nations," or people groups. Not just individuals or families or cities, but *nations*. For the first time in my ministry, I asked a totally different question: "How can I obey the Great Commission by discipling a whole nation for God?"

When one draws a circle around the borders of a nation with the intention of discipling that whole nation, it doesn't take long to realize that the most strategic person in that nation is the president or king. But how could I ever hope to even *meet* the many leaders of Africa?

Yet when I was training ninety-five hundred leaders in Nigeria, I found myself invited to lunch with the president of the nation, who told me that everywhere he traveled in the world, someone would give him a copy of *The Prayer of Jabez* and that the book had changed his life.

Then when I was in Zambia training more than seven hundred leaders, the president of that nation invited me to his office and told me he had just finished reading *The Prayer of Jabez*—twice. He came around his large desk and asked me to place my hands on his shoulders and pray for him.

Later I was to speak with the president and first lady of Uganda to find out firsthand how they had achieved a remarkable turnaround and stemmed the tide of HIV infection in their nation. The president was unexpectedly called north to an outbreak of fighting, but his wife gave me the warmest welcome and said, "Oh, we love *The Prayer of Jabez*! But *Secrets of the Vine* is my favorite."

As of this writing, I have just returned from Malawi,

where we were launching another Dream for Africa ministry. Just before we were to fly back to Johannesburg, we received word that the first lady of Malawi wanted to meet with us. As we were introduced, the first lady's adult daughter enthusiastically said to her mother, "This is the man I've been telling you about, the one who wrote the book I just gave you!"

One leader said to me recently, "*The Prayer of Jabez* is your John the Baptist for your work in Africa!"

Who could have guessed?

WHY ANOTHER BOOK ABOUT JABEZ?

If you were inspired by *The Prayer of Jabez*, or even if you've never heard of it, my hope is that this book will deeply encourage you and enable you to live at a new level of meaning, service, and significance. As I have been praying this little prayer for more than thirty years, my heart is overflowing with not only my own experiences but also how God has answered this prayer for untold millions of people around the world, and so I have shared a number of their stories in these pages.

But *Beyond Jabez* was written for three primary reasons.

First, I wrote it to further develop the concepts in this prayer so that they can produce even more fruit in your life. The original book was only a brief overview of the prayer, and so many people have asked for additional teaching on the topic. In response, I developed an eight-part small-group video series (available at www.brucewilkinson.com) and now this book.

Second, I wrote *Beyond Jabez* to clear up some of the

misconceptions that have arisen out of the success of the first book. Frankly, the amount of false teaching and preaching that surrounded the book came as a complete shock to me. Why? Because in twenty-five years of preaching on the prayer of Jabez, I never heard one negative comment. And no one ever even suggested that asking God to bless you was prosperity gospel. Only after *The Prayer of Jabez* became a runaway bestseller did I begin to hear this kind of criticism. The secular press, in particular, had a difficult time handling the overwhelming success of a book on prayer.

The third reason I wrote this new book was to encourage you to rekindle the habit of praying the prayer of Jabez. So many have been touched and their lives changed, but the Jabez experience is hardly over; in fact, it's just beginning!

Rarely does a week go by when we don't see numerous instances of God's answering this prayer in our family's lives and at Dream for Africa. My good friend and publisher, Don Jacobson, encouraged me to include in this book a number of these stories from the past few months, just so readers would see and understand that the prayer of Jabez can be an ongoing part of a vital and effective prayer life.

A LIFE THAT IS MORE HONORABLE

Just as you ask God to bless your food, my hope is that after reading *Beyond Jabez*, you will make it your habit to ask God to bless you. Then, as you come to realize that your life is meant to be ever growing in its influence and impact, I hope you will ask God daily for more territory in which to serve Him. This will lead you into the Land of the Unknown, where you may feel overwhelmed and perhaps even incapable of handling the opportunities; if so, I hope you will pray as Jabez did for the hand of the Lord to intervene on your behalf. Finally, when the reality of life on another plane causes your heart to falter—leaving you vulnerable to temptation that, if acted on, would hurt the Lord and others and stop the miracles you've been experiencing—my hope is you will know to ask the Lord to keep evil from you so that you will not cause pain.

In this book, you will discover the power of this unbroken linkage. And if you will pray the prayer of Jabez and live according to its biblical principles, you too will discover the indescribable joy of experiencing the words, "And God granted him that which he requested."

As you lose yourself in serving the King, you may find to your surprise that heaven describes you, as it did Jabez, as "more honorable." I'm convinced, from Scripture and personal experience, that Jabez revealed one of the remarkable secrets of a life that is honorable before God and man. May your heart sing and your life explode with the joys of living in the fullness that lies potentially before you.

CHAPTER ONE

CATCH GOD'S DREAM!

Not long ago and not far away, a Nobody named
Ordinary lived in the Land of Familiar.
For the most part, not much happened in Familiar that
hadn't happened before. Ordinary thought he was content.
He found the routines reliable. He blended in with the crowd.
And mostly, he wanted only what he had.
Until the day Ordinary noticed a small, nagging
feeling that something big was missing from his life.[1]

THE DREAM GIVER

I need twenty-five volunteers," Pastor Denny Bellesi
announced to his unsuspecting congregation. He scanned the
packed auditorium for responses.

The members of Coast Hills Community Church sat in
puzzled silence.

What in the world was their pastor up to now? Worshipers
slouched in their seats, trying to look inconspicuous.

Eventually, twenty-five curious people stood before the

congregation—some willingly, some reluctantly. The pastor then handed each a crisp $100 bill.

"I invite you to take part in this Kingdom Assignment," he told the astounded volunteers. "The rules are simple. One, this is not your money; it is God's. Two, you are to use this money to further God's kingdom beyond the four walls of the church. And three, you must report back in ninety days and share with everyone how you invested the money."

He further surprised his congregation by announcing that the church didn't want a penny of this money back. He repeated the exercise in the following three worship services, eventually distributing $10,000 to one hundred members of his church. Men, women, and even children were recipients of this "investment cash."

Pastor Bellesi had recently finished preaching a series about how to use money for God's purposes. He felt that his church was ready—financially and spiritually—to take on the exciting challenge of investing in God's kingdom.

What began as a simple lesson in stewardship for one church is still touching lives around the world.

Denny knew the risk he was taking. He was well aware of the unusual responsibility that he had placed on his congregation. But the people rose to the challenge, and the Kingdom Assignment impacted more lives than anyone anticipated. What began as a simple lesson in stewardship for one church is still touching lives around the world.

One man raised $10,000 by sending e-mails to friends and old classmates, challenging them to match the original $100 amount. He donated the funds to a couple whose two young daughters had just died from a rare blood disorder.

A woman told several friends about the Kingdom Assignment during a birthday celebration. She and her enthused companions raised $1,800 and donated the cash to a struggling single mother of three, who worked during the day and attended college at night.

A nine-year-old girl sent her money to a four-year-old girl in Oregon to help pay for the ailing child's heart surgery.

A local chiropractor elected to take his portable massage table and a hundred Burger King hamburgers down to skid row once a month and adjust the aching backs of those who live and sleep on the streets.

Another man was inspired to invest $50,000 in a Bible seminary in China after hearing about the Kingdom Assignment.

One young man who had grown up in an abusive home invested his money in a mentoring program for abused kids. He also participates in the program, which has helped him discover a part of God's purpose for his life.

Just a few weeks after giving his congregation their Kingdom Assignment, Pastor Bellesi read *The Prayer of Jabez* and it impacted him deeply. He then gave copies to all his staff. Denny Bellesi and his wife, Leesa, began to pray together, asking the Lord to "expand their territory." They had no idea that their territory was about to explode.

First, a regional newspaper caught wind of the good deeds coming out of the church and ran a feature story on their front page. Soon after, the Associated Press picked up the story, and papers around the world printed the heartwarming tale. *Woman's Day* and *People* magazines wrote articles about the wonderful happenings as a result of the Kingdom Assignment. Denny and Leesa began receiving calls from all over the world with requests for magazine and radio interviews.

And their territory just kept expanding.

One day, the Bellesis got a phone call from an associate producer with NBC's *Dateline*. She asked if they could follow the story for a year. Denny and Leesa agreed, so a film crew showed up at the church to interview Denny and several of the Kingdom Assignment participants. The church members made the most of the opportunity to expand God's territory by sharing what God had done for them.

In the midst of this flurry of activity, Leesa wrote a proposal for a book chronicling the results of the Kingdom Assignment. Leesa and Denny soon landed a book contract with a major Christian publisher.

The Bellesis were so overwhelmed by the enormity of God's blessings that they were being forced to depend on God. And that was good! The Kingdom Assignment had become so big that only God could take the credit.

Like the proverbial pebble making ripples in the pond, the impact of the Kingdom Assignment continues to spread. These ripples have touched the lives of people in many countries, including Sudan, China, Vietnam, and Mexico.

And it shows no sign of losing momentum.[2]

NEVER TOO LATE

Since the publication of *The Prayer of Jabez* in 2000, I have received numerous letters with stories of how God has used people who prayed with the faith of Jabez. Like the Kingdom Assignment, some of these are big, splashy stories of spectacular miracles from the hand of God. But many of God's miracles happen in quieter, but no less eternally significant, fashion.

Let me tell you about a special seventy-year-old lady named Mamie. Her faith in God had always been strong. But when declining health required that her family place her in an assisted-living home, Mamie began to manifest negative traits they had never seen before—resentment, suspicion, emotional withdrawal. Her children wondered what had happened to the woman who had raised them.

About this time, Mamie's daughter JoAn read *The Prayer of Jabez*. She was encouraged by its teaching and became convinced that her mother needed the perspective it provided. The irony was that, all her life, JoAn could remember her mother frequently exhorting the family, "Trust the Lord to enlarge your territory." But JoAn had never known the source of the quote. Until now.

The next time she visited her mother, JoAn was shocked to see the bitterness and despair etched into Mamie's face. The ailing woman felt she had lost everything of importance—her home, her possessions, her independence— and was certain she had nothing left to live for.

Mamie's expression began to change, however, as JoAn reminded her mother of the perspective Mamie had spent her life teaching her children: God is faithful and He loves to give; He will be with us as we step out boldly in faithful obedience.

JoAn read 1 Chronicles 4:10 to her mother: "And Jabez called on the God of Israel saying, 'Oh, that You would bless me indeed, and enlarge my territory, that Your hand would be with me, and that You would keep me from evil, that I may not cause pain!' So God granted him what he requested."

"Yes," said Mamie softly, as though talking to herself. "That's what He does."

"Mom, God has set you right in the midst of people who

need you," JoAn said. "Here you are with thirteen other women, all under the same roof. You've spent your whole life influencing others for good. I'm not going to just stand by and watch the devil rob you of your joy and ministry during the last years of your life!"

At that, Mamie smiled for what may have been the first time in months.

JoAn challenged her mother to share with her fellow residents what she had learned about God's love throughout her seven decades of life. They prayed together for God's direction and strength, and by the time JoAn left, Mamie was a new woman with new purpose.

Many of God's miracles happen in quieter, but no less eternally significant, fashion.

A few days later, Mamie called JoAn and asked her to bring cookies and tea for a meeting she had organized. She had invited a Christian friend named Esther to come speak to her fellow residents in the nursing home's living area.

On the day of the event, anticipation shone on each woman's face as a parade of thirteen walkers and wheelchairs made its way down the corridor. Not one of them could remember the last time they had been invited for tea!

The atmosphere in the home was transformed. Esther's sharing and then a series of subsequent events—including a mini-concert by Mamie's grandchildren—brought hope and new faith into the lives of several of the elderly ladies.

Some time later, when Mamie became gravely ill with congestive heart failure, she was certain she was on her way to heaven. But when her condition improved, she told JoAn, "I guess God isn't finished with me yet. There must be something more He wants me to do."[3]

Whether you have six days or sixty years remaining, God still has you here on earth for a purpose. I pray that this book will help you catch the vision for what God wants to do in your life, that you will experience incredible fulfillment and produce results of eternal value.

JABEZ THE MAN

You'll notice in both of these stories that people were already learning to trust God to see His hand of power in their lives even before *The Prayer of Jabez* came to their attention. In fact, Jabez's prayer has been in our Bibles, influencing people's lives for thousands of years, and it will still be there long after the little book I've written has crumbled to dust and been forgotten. People have been praying Jabez's prayer and living by these principles for centuries, but God has seen fit in the last few years to let Jabez's example change millions of lives around the world—perhaps including yours.

So let's take a moment to look again at the man whose heart of faith has made such an impact in our day. In the book of 1 Chronicles, we find only two verses about Jabez, nestled in the middle of a long list of names—within the genealogy of no less a personage than King David himself. The second of these verses contains Jabez's prayer. But if we step back one verse, we learn more about the man and his circumstances: "Now Jabez was more honorable than his brothers, and his mother called his name Jabez, saying, 'Because I bore him in pain'" (1 Chronicles 4:9).

First, note the meaning of his name. The word *jabez* literally means "pain." Maybe his mother had difficulty giving birth. Or maybe other painful circumstances overwhelmed her at that time. In any case, imagine growing up and hearing over and over, "Hey, Pain! What's up?" Or introducing yourself, "Hi, everyone. I'm Pain." No doubt the boy had some significant obstacles to overcome before he developed into a man of strong faith! Jabez's legacy has encouraged millions whose lives started in pain, teaching them that they can overcome their circumstances and become a person whom God calls "honorable."

Jabez serves as a worthy example for us to follow even today.

Indeed, Jabez was known to be "more honorable than his brothers." The word *honorable* as used here means "respected." Jabez lived in such a way—with maturity, wisdom, and a sense of honor—that he stood out from the crowd. He was admired for all the right reasons. And so he serves as a worthy example for us to follow even today.

We also learn from this passage that Jabez "called on the God of Israel." The word *call* here means "to cry out for help." The prayer of Jabez was not an off-the-cuff inquiry ("Oh, Lord, by the way..."); his was a heartfelt, passionate plea. Given what we're told about Jabez in the Bible, I think we can infer that this prayer represented an overriding theme in his life—a constant, deep desire.

A P A S S I O N S O G R E A T...

Have you ever wanted anything that badly? For a moment, try to imagine a desire so intense that it drives everything else from your consciousness. Then imagine asking God, day after day with fervent intensity, to fulfill in your life four very specific yet seemingly audacious requests.

Imagine that you long for God's *blessing*—spiritual or material, or both—abundantly poured out, according to His eternal riches and generous wisdom.

And then, as He pours out His blessing on your life, imagine aspiring to take new *territory*—not primarily for yourself, but for Him and His purposes.

And as your borders expand and the responsibility God entrusts to you grows to the point that it becomes overwhelming, picture yourself crying out desperately for His *hand of power* to enable you to steward the responsibility well.

Now consider that under these conditions you might become so sensitive to sin's destructive effect that you plead with God, *Keep me from evil!* so that you might pursue His best for your life without hindrance.

If you can begin to grasp this passion, this mind-set, this wondrous habit of faith-filled prayer, then you've already started to expand your borders into the next stage of God's adventure for you.

BLESSING FROM GOD

And Jabez called on the God of Israel saying,
"Oh, that You would bless me indeed,
and enlarge my territory,
that Your hand would be with me,
and that You would keep me from evil,
that I may not cause pain!"
So God granted him what he requested.

1 CHRONICLES 4:10

MOURNING INTO DANCING

by Cathy Davis

It was not a good year.

After twenty-two years of marriage, I was alone. I had lost both my house and my car. My son seemed bent on self-destruction through alcohol and drug abuse. And as if that weren't enough pain for one year, my beloved dog died.

But I picked up the pieces and labored to earn a college degree, determined to land my dream job.

It didn't take long for that bubble to burst. Once in the job market, I learned that the wages available for my level of experience—or, should I say, inexperience—weren't nearly enough to make ends meet. I took a risk and started a business. Which failed.

No matter how I tried, I felt as though I kept sliding back to the bottom of the heap of life.

I had already been fasting and praying that God would give me more of Himself—the greatest blessing of all. And now, my every plan thwarted, I opened myself completely to

His direction: *I'm in a desperate place, Lord. I want You to quiet my heart so that I can hear Your will for my life. My plans haven't taken me anywhere. Please bless me...the way You choose.*

For some time I sought the Lord, hoping He would just write the answers on the wall, as He had done in the Bible for Daniel the prophet. But He simply kept me clinging more and more desperately to the promise of His goodness.

Finally, while I was fasting, I thought I sensed God's leading, and with no tuition money in hand, I began to apply to complete my master's degree at the local university. I was told early in the process that all grants had already been claimed, that there were no jobs available, and that even the academic adviser I had requested would be gone on sabbatical.

But God gave me peace. If this was His plan for my life, it would somehow come to pass; He would work out the details. So I finished applying for admission and financial aid.

The next day—only ten days after I had prayed for God's choice of blessing and direction—I received a call from the graduate school dean. "Cathy, I just wanted you to know you've been accepted into our graduate program. I believe we can help you with finances as well."

In fact, I received a full scholarship, with a stipend for teaching, and a part-time job. What's more, the adviser I had requested canceled her sabbatical and was now available!

Throughout my life, my heavenly Father has never ceased to be the One who loves to give and to bless. But it was when I asked Him for abundant blessing—according to His plan, not mine—that He showered down all I needed and more.

THE PRAYER FOR
BLESSING:
A CLOSER LOOK

God really does have unclaimed blessings waiting for you,
my friend. I know it sounds impossible—
even embarrassingly suspicious in our self-serving day.
Yet that very exchange—your want for God's plenty—
has been His loving will for your life from eternity past.[1]

THE PRAYER OF JABEZ

*T*he *Prayer of Jabez* was almost aborted before I even
dreamed of writing about it.

I first thought of praying this little prayer more than
thirty years ago when the chaplain at our graduate school
mentioned this little-known Old Testament hero and
challenged us, as students, to aspire to become as he was—
that is, "more honorable." I can remember gulping at this as

an impressionable graduate student, almost hoping against hope that becoming more honorable held even the slightest possibility for me.

That chapel so affected me that I did not dash to the snack room for my usual morning coffee and doughnut, but instead headed straight for the library. There I ransacked the shelves, pulling down several large Bible dictionaries, commentaries, and reference tools. I wanted to find out everything there was to know about this man who had so captured my imagination.

Here's what I found:

> Now Jabez was more honorable than his brothers, and his mother called his name Jabez, saying, "Because I bore him in pain."
>
> And Jabez called on the God of Israel saying, "Oh, that You would bless me indeed, and enlarge my territory, that Your hand would be with me, and that You would keep me from evil, that I may not cause pain!" So God granted him what he requested.
>
> 1 CHRONICLES 4:9–10

I can't tell you how disappointed I was to discover that Jabez only appeared in these two all-too-short verses. How could I ever hope to become like him if the Bible never revealed his secrets? Sitting back in that hard wooden library chair, my heart wrestled with frustration. *Why didn't God tell us more about Jabez?*

I kept reading verse 9 time after time, hoping that something I hadn't seen would leap off the page at me. Finally, I began to wonder about his prayer, and an odd thought came to me: *Why not pray his prayer?* It made sense. In various worship services I had been part of, the congregation had prayed *other* people's prayers, so why not Jabez's?

It appeared to be so simple. Until I tried to pray it.

The words just stuck in my throat and I couldn't get them out, no matter how hard I tried. "Dear God, please bless...me?" You aren't supposed to pray that way. Everyone knows that you're supposed to pray for the sick and for the minister. But to pray for yourself? No way! It felt like the most selfish prayer I could think of.

My mind raced, trying to make sense of this unexpected contradiction. How could a person whom the Bible described as "more honorable than his brethren" (KJV) ever pray so selfishly? The more I sat there and studied the passage, the more uncomfortable I became.

I wanted to examine this more deeply, so I took out my pad and wrote out the four very different parts of Jabez's prayer. Not only was I uncomfortable with his first request, but I found each one was exactly the opposite of what I had prayed all my life. Instead of asking for "more territory" I was always complaining that I had too much territory and wishing that He would take some of it away; I already had far too much work to do. Instead of praying for His hand of power, I tried to avoid any situations that might place me in a predicament where I would need to depend on God's supernatural intervention. After all, did God really do such things anyway? Not in my life.

"And God granted him that which he requested."

The more I read the prayer, the more I couldn't put it together. How could Jabez pray like that? It was clearly wrong.

Wrong, that is, until I read the last part of that verse: "And God granted him that which he requested" (KJV).

God isn't in the habit of answering selfish prayers. James 4:3 tells us, "You ask and do not receive, because you ask amiss, that you may spend it on your pleasures." And yet God granted Jabez what he asked for. Could it be that we are *supposed* to ask for God's blessing? Could it be that a person who is more honorable in God's eyes will pray this way?

I took a deep breath, hoped no one could hear me, and then forced myself to ask the Lord, "Please bless me indeed!"

God answered Jabez's prayer for blessing, and He continues to answer with remarkable gifts of His grace and kindness. That's why I prayed the Jabez prayer even this morning.

JUDY SAW THE LIGHT

Not only is the Lord generous, but He also manifests boundless creativity in the ways He chooses to pour out His blessings. Judy learned this the night she and her husband, Jeff, were driving home through Montana near the end of their vacation. While Jeff snoozed in the passenger seat, Judy decided to make the most of the time by conversing with her heavenly Father.

Lord, if this prayer of Jabez is for us today, please show me. She paused, then prayed, *Lord, bless me indeed.*

Nothing dramatic happened immediately, but Judy began to consider what form God's answer might take. Then she glanced over at her sleeping husband. *Yes, that would be a blessing,* she thought, *that Jeff would commit his life to You. It couldn't get much better than that.*

That's when she first noticed the luminous glow in the northern sky. Judy knew they were far from any large cities, and dawn was hours away. The sky brightened and began to dance with streaks of red and orange and green, and Judy woke Jeff to see the rare display of the aurora borealis, the northern lights. Jeff insisted they pull over and they sat watching their own private light show for two hours.

Finally, Jeff took Judy's hand and said, "We need to pray."

Judy's eyes welled with tears as Jeff responded to God's glorious display: "Thank You, Lord, for this beautiful blessing You've given us."

Judy added her silent thanks for God's prompt answer to her request.

Soon after the cosmic light show, Jeff attended church with Judy and shared with the congregation how God had revealed His spectacular majesty that night. A few weeks later he gave his life fully to Jesus Christ.[2]

To Judy's great joy—and to God's delight—she discovered the abundant generosity of God's giving heart. She took seriously His prompting to ask for blessing. And for Judy and Jeff the results will last for eternity.

JABEZ'S FIRST REQUEST

By the time he prayed the prayer recorded in the Old Testament, Jabez had apparently also come to appreciate God's generosity. He knew the One who loves to give. So he mustered the boldness to petition the God of Israel, "Oh, that You would bless me indeed" (1 Chronicles 4:10).

The Hebrew word for *bless* means "to bestow favor or kindness." So when Jabez said, "Bless me indeed," he was asking God, "Would You please pour out Your goodness upon me?" And though God's blessings come in many forms, neither Jabez nor God was embarrassed that His answer might be material or financial.

But there's another element of Jabez's request we can't afford to miss. It's that last word, *indeed*. In the original Hebrew language, in which the Old Testament is written, we find no separate word for *indeed*. Rather, in Hebrew grammar the writer had the option of slightly changing the spelling of the verb in order to add the meaning *intensely* or *immensely*. The effect is similar to when we take a bland statement like "I broke the mirror" and crank up the amplification to say instead, "I smashed the mirror into a million pieces!" That's what the writer of 1 Chronicles did with the verb for *bless*; he changed the word's form in order to make it mean *bless intensely*. Jabez was saying, "God, I really want You to bless me—not just a little, but a lot!"

Not only do many of us find it difficult to ask God to bless us, but asking for a "big blessing" can be even more uncomfortable. Somehow, it feels selfish. Selfish with a capital S.

After I taught on this principle a few years ago, a man came up to me, visibly upset about the notion of asking God for a blessing. He got even more worked up when I pointed out that Jabez didn't want a little blessing, he wanted a big blessing. The man couldn't contain himself a moment longer. "That's wrong!" he shouted.

I prayed for wisdom and picked up seven books from the top of a nearby piano. I then made three piles. The first pile had one book, the second two books, and the third had four books.

"Each of these represents blessings from the Lord," I said. "The size of the pile represents the size of the blessing. Which one would you like?"

The man turned red with frustration and with tight lips mumbled, "The biggest one."

I smiled and assured him that's the pile any of us would choose. Then I said, "Let's say that you're a game show contestant and you win the grand prize. You have a choice of three prizes: a new refrigerator, a new car, and a new house. Which one would you choose?"

He laughed and said, "The house, of course!"

"But sir, you are so selfish!" I exclaimed. The truth had slipped in the back door.

He blurted out, "But I would be a fool to ask for the smallest one!"

WELL-TIMED GENEROSITY

A woman named Christine learned to pray for God's abundant blessing, but only after many years of self-inflicted pain. Addicted to intravenous cocaine and running from her second marriage, she finally found refuge with her brother Marty and his wife, Tracy, who were pastoring a church in Nashville.

Marty challenged Christine to give God a chance to work in her life. And although she doubted God's ability to forgive her for all she had done, she accepted the opportunity and settled in at her brother's church. One of God's first blessings was the restoration of Christine's marriage. Her husband, Mickey, moved to Nashville soon after and they started a new life together.

About this time, Christine accepted the challenge to pray for thirty days as Jabez had prayed, to see what God might do in her life. She made a calendar and carefully charted her progress. Though she knew that her deep financial indebtedness was her own doing, she and Mickey asked God specifically to help them make a fresh financial start.

One afternoon a month later, a FedEx employee came to the door and handed Christine an envelope. She ripped it open and took out a check for $73,600! The money was compensation for a forgotten work-related injury she had suffered six years before.

Her shrieks of joy brought Marty running. "Look!" she hollered, waving the check in his face. "I can't believe they sent the money after all these years."

Upon reflection, Christine realized that the timing of God's blessing had proven to be an even greater expression of His love. Had He provided the check any earlier, while Christine was still mired in her old lifestyle, she would have spent the money on drugs, perhaps even at the expense of her life.[3]

Distinctives of the Prayer for Blessing

Lord, bless me indeed. There has been a lot of heated debate and discussion over the past few years about what exactly this part of the prayer means and what it does *not* mean. Let me try to bring the issues into focus with a few clarifying distinctions.

First, the prayer is not impersonal, but personal. Jabez didn't ask, "Please bless the world," but rather, "Please bless *me*." And unapologetically so. Praying for the world is good, but so is praying for yourself.

Second, the prayer is not specific, but general. God's blessing is, by definition, directed and determined by God, not by man. If you limit your expectations and request to one specific way you want God to bless you, you may be praying a valid prayer, but you're no longer praying with the open heart of Jabez. Ultimately, there's only One who knows the most appropriate and fulfilling blessing for you, and that's God. Trust Him.

Third, the prayer does not ask for meager provision, but for abundant blessing. Do you think your heavenly Father is stingy? When we ask for great blessing, He will choose wisely how and when to answer, but He is not put off by enthusiastic prayer. In fact, if our great passion is an expression of great honesty and fervor, then God welcomes it.

Fourth, the prayer doesn't limit the request to a specific time, like "today," but allows God to bless whenever, wherever, and however He prefers. Too often, we are tempted to put a time limit on the Lord. True, many of the prayers of the Bible specify a time limit—for example, Jehoshaphat prays for the people of Israel when the massive Syrian armies are preparing to attack the next morning—but Jabez's prayer does not. If you ask, "Please, Lord, bless me by next Friday," you are no longer praying the prayer of Jabez.

Do you want God's blessing enough to ask for it?

Which leads to our fifth distinction: *The prayer is not a weak wish, but a fervent desire.* Have you ever found yourself cheering wildly at a sporting event—maybe one in which your son or daughter was playing, where the score was extremely close? Remember the feeling of adrenaline pumping through your veins? Perhaps you cheered yourself hoarse, or maybe you clenched your fists so tightly your fingernails left deep impressions in your palms. This is the degree of desire with which Jabez prayed.

Do *you* want God's blessing enough to ask for it? To ask for it with hunger and urgency?

I freely admit that the prayer for blessing runs contrary to the way many of us have been taught to pray—as does each part of the prayer of Jabez. Because praying for abundant blessing seems so unusual in modern Christian practice, a number of misconceptions about the prayer of Jabez have arisen since the release of the book in 2000. I want to deal with three of them here.

MISCONCEPTION # 1: MAGICAL PRAYING

A lady once came up to me and said, "Dr. Wilkinson, thank you so much for your book." She continued enthusiastically, "I've stopped praying everything else. I'm only praying Jabez. It's amazing how it works. It's like magic!"

I paused for a moment, then said, "Ma'am, would you do something for me? Would you please burn my book?"

She, like a few others, had succumbed to a common misconception about praying for God's blessing:

> BLESSING MISCONCEPTION # 1:
> *The prayer of Jabez always works—*
> *just say the words.*

The truth is, The prayer of Jabez is not magic. It's a prayer—an expression of your heart to God's. Don't construe the specific words of the prayer as some kind of incantation or formula to which God is obligated to respond. Rather, look to Jabez's heart attitude as a model to follow.

When you pray as Jabez did, your whole person is mobilized in genuine relationship with God; it's not just your lips issuing a few meaningless words. In fact, when I pray the prayer of Jabez, I rarely use his exact words but instead follow the four basic themes of the original prayer: I ask God to bless me a great deal, to expand my territory or sphere of influence, to provide His hand of power in my life, and to keep me from evil and temptation.

That said, I am fully confident that the Lord answers this prayer, whatever the words. Why? Because it's effective! Numerous pastors from around the world have told me the same thing about what *The Prayer of Jabez* did for their congregations: "That little book did more to help my people to pray than anything I've ever seen. Nearly everyone in our church had a testimony of what God did when they prayed the prayer."

Why does it work? As you will soon see, each of the four parts of the prayer correspond with the teachings of the Bible, including those of Jesus Himself. In other words, the prayer of Jabez works because you are asking God to help you do the very things that Christ commanded you to do. You never have to wonder if the prayer is right to pray—it is the will of God as revealed by Jesus Christ! As you will soon see, it may be an Old Testament prayer, but it reflects New Testament truths.

Whenever I'm teaching this to young people, I use this overly simplistic illustration: Let's say that your mother has already told you that you are responsible to clean up the kitchen after supper each night this week. Yet each night as you finish your dessert, you plead with Mom, "Please, *please* let me clear the table and wash the dishes!" What do you suppose your mother will say?

Think about it for a moment. Jesus commanded us to "go

therefore and make disciples of all the nations" (Matthew 28:19). Jabez prayed, "Enlarge my territory." He wanted more influence, more responsibility, more opportunity to make a mark for the God of Israel. So if you're praying, "God, please let me do more for you; expand my influence for you," you are asking God to let you do the *very* thing He has commanded you to do.

Does God answer prayers from people seeking to obey? Absolutely.

But by no means is this the only prayer you should pray. In fact, it's the *last* thing I pray during my time with God. I urge you to follow the example of Jabez, but never apart from a life-encompassing conversation with God.

MISCONCEPTION # 2: SELFISH PRAYING

The second misconception is one with which I struggled during my early encounters with Jabez. At first, like many, praying for myself felt downright wrong.

> BLESSING MISCONCEPTION # 2:
> *I can't pray the prayer of Jabez.*
> *It's not right to pray for myself.*

The truth is, the prayer of Jabez is *not* a selfish prayer. And it *is* right to pray for yourself. How can this be so?

Let's imagine that God has a box in heaven containing a limited number of blessings that He will dispense each day. And being a morning person, I rise at the crack of dawn and start praying, "Lord, please give me a lot of blessings."

God says, "That's fine with Me, son. You're here early, so have all you want."

Then my friend Fred, being something of a night owl, rolls out of bed a couple of hours later and prays the same: "Lord, please bless me a lot."

But this time God replies, "I'm sorry, Fred. I wish I could, but unfortunately, I gave all of today's blessings to Wilkinson."

If this were the case, then it would be selfish of me to pray for abundant blessing, since I would be depriving someone else. But in fact, there are no limits on God's capacity to bless us, so how can I hurt you if I pray for myself? I can't. It's impossible.

In fact, when God grants me abundant blessing, my surplus makes it easier for me to *bless* you. This is true with all of God's gifts, but it is particularly true of intangible blessings, such as love, acceptance, and assurance. When God fills my heart to overflowing, I have more inner resources for encouraging those who feel unloved and insecure.

Sharing God's blessing was the desire that motivated Anne and her three children as the kids prepared to go on summer mission trips. With their fund-raising deadline only weeks away, Ashleigh, Christina, and Andrew still needed $6,000 between them. They had sent letters to friends and family requesting support, but their account balance sat at only $60.

Anne used this opportunity to teach her children to ask for God's blessing and to trust Him for their needs. All four of them started to pray. And that's when the money began pouring in from sources they never expected. They even received $100 from their coffee vendor!

Thanks to God's provision, the children departed with

faith-strengthened hearts for Florida, France, and Vanuatu in the South Pacific. There they served as overflowing vessels of God's abundant blessing. They had asked to be blessed, but they had asked with the needs of others in mind.[4]

MISCONCEPTION #3: GET-RICH-QUICK SCHEME

A third misconception has arisen because of the way some people (to my astonishment) have used the prayer of Jabez to support prosperity theology—that is, the teaching that if you pray or speak in a certain way, God will make you rich.

BLESSING MISCONCEPTION #3:
If you want to get rich, pray the prayer of Jabez.

The truth is, *The Prayer of Jabez* does not teach prosperity gospel. Scripture clearly teaches that many of God's faithful will endure hardship and poverty while receiving abundant spiritual blessing and the promise of great reward in eternity (see Matthew 10:21–40; John 16:33).

I call this "the Jabez Firestorm" because this issue became the most misunderstood and widely disseminated misconception in the wake of the book's popularity. If you had told me beforehand that someone would twist the prayer of Jabez into a get-rich-quick scheme, I would never have believed you. In fact, it never even entered my mind until I read the first review from an antagonistic secular magazine writer. You could have knocked me over with a feather! I was stunned and heartsick.

You might wonder why this interpretation came as such a surprise to me. There are three reasons. First, before writing the book I had preached the message of Jabez for more than twenty-five years in churches, Bible colleges, seminaries, and leadership conferences in dozens of nations around the world. In all those years, I never once heard one negative comment about the message. Not one. In fact, I preached the prayer of Jabez as my senior sermon at Dallas Theological Seminary. (I got an A.)

Second, I am opposed to the prosperity gospel and the extravagant lifestyle that has often accompanied its teachings. I have ministered on many topics in many locations and never once to my knowledge ever taught or exemplified the prosperity gospel teachings or values.

Third, I specifically dismissed any connection between the prosperity gospel and the prayer of Jabez on page 24 of the book. Read the passage carefully and see for yourself. Maybe it isn't as clear as I thought it was:

> Notice a radical aspect of Jabez's request for blessing: He left it entirely up to God to decide what the blessings would be and where, when, and how Jabez would receive them.
>
> This kind of radical trust in God's good intentions toward us has nothing in common with the popular gospel that you should ask God for a Cadillac, a six-figure income, or some other material sign that you have found a way to cash in on your connection with Him. Instead, the Jabez blessing focuses like a laser on our wanting nothing more and nothing less than what God wants for us.

It was while my family was on vacation in Florida that I realized how far some people had taken the prayer of Jabez out of context for their own purposes. As we were checking out of a local grocery store, our younger daughter, Jessica, burst out, "Dad, look at that! That magazine is advertising the Prayer of Jabez Shield." A pause. "Dad, what's the Prayer of Jabez Shield?"

"I don't know, sweetheart."

"But I thought you wrote the book on Jabez?"

I followed her pointing finger, and there it was, advertised on the front of a tabloid. My curiosity piqued, I surreptitiously bought a copy of the magazine and examined it in the parking lot. Inside the magazine, within a dotted outline in the shape of a shield, was printed the prayer of Jabez. The accompanying instructions told readers to cut out the shield and paste it onto cardboard backing. They could then use the shield in a variety of ways. They might buy a lottery ticket, then place the Prayer of Jabez Shield on top of it, and they were sure to win. Or an unmarried person might write a list of ten qualities in his ideal mate, place the shield on top of the list, put them both under his pillow at night, and God would provide the perfect partner within days.

This kind of pseudo-theology is an affront to the God of truth and to the millions of faithful Christians worldwide who endure physical poverty and illness, despite their great faith. Jabez didn't believe this way, and neither do I.

DEALING WITH YOUR DISCOMFORT

Does the idea of asking God to pour out His abundance still bother you? If so, you're not alone. I struggled with the idea for a long time. But in the next chapter we will see that God actually *commands* us to seek His blessing.

Before we go there, though, look with me briefly at a man named Jacob. According to Genesis 32:22–29, one night the Angel of the Lord appeared to Jacob, who didn't recognize Him. Jacob literally wrestled with God all night long. As dawn broke, Jacob had the audacity to demand, "I will not let You go unless You bless me!"

God's response? He blessed Jacob.

He didn't have to. Most theologians agree that Jacob wasn't living a particularly holy or God-honoring life at the time. Yet God blessed him.

May we all, like this bold man, grow to desire God's abundant generosity enough to overcome our reluctance and ask.

CHAPTER THREE

THE PRAYER FOR BLESSING: GOING DEEPER

"Ask, and it will be given to you;
seek, and you will find; knock, and it will be opened to you.
For everyone who asks receives, and he who seeks finds,
and to him who knocks it will be opened."

MATTHEW 7:7–8

Histoplasmosis. Patsy couldn't pronounce it, but she finally had a name for her malady.

Her eye specialist continued explaining the rare condition, which is usually contracted from bird droppings. Patsy had apparently picked it up from the chicken farm near where she used to live.

The prognosis? Here, the doctor hesitated. "The vision in your right eye is so far gone that there's not much we can do.

But we can keep a close watch on your left eye."

This was not the news Patsy had hoped for, but she thanked God for the vision in her good eye and moved on with her life.

Several years later her husband, Don, was diagnosed with terminal cancer. During his decline Patsy realized she was losing sight in her left eye. She accepted this as perhaps God's way of keeping her home to care for her husband, and they made the most of their time together.

After Don passed away, Patsy's sight deteriorated to the point that she could no longer drive or even read. Eventually, she was unable to recognize other people's faces. Patsy felt like a prisoner in her own home.

One day a friend stopped by and gave Patsy a copy of *The Prayer of Jabez*. She took out her strongest magnifying glass and labored to read the small print. Bit by bit, as she read, hope began to dawn in her heart. She stopped and prayed, "Father, could You possibly want to bless me by restoring my sight?" Patsy had been legally blind for nearly a decade, yet this was the first time she had prayed for healing. Hesitant to ask for too much, she continued, "I'm going to ask You to restore sight to my left eye, Lord. That's all I need to get by."

She brought this request before God daily. At first, the change was almost imperceptible. Then one morning Patsy could make out her hands. The next day she could see the movement of her fingers. Soon she could recognize her friends and family by their faces, not just by their voices.

Patsy could barely contain her laughter when her eye doctor examined her, shaking his head in amazement. "Your left eye has gone from 20/400 to 20/40," he said.

She kept praying, and soon she got back her driver's license. And she can't stop telling others what God has done for her.[1]

BLESSINGS SURROUND US

Did you notice that even before her healing Patsy recognized and thanked God for His blessings? When she learned what was wrong with her right eye, she thanked God for the sight in her left. When her left eye began to degrade, she appreciated the opportunity to stay home with her dying husband.

Somehow, earlier in life, Patsy learned a very important principle that is related to the Jabez prayer: *Every blessing, large or small, is from God.*

In James 1:16–17 we read, "Do not be deceived, my beloved brethren. Every good gift and every perfect gift is from above, and comes down from the Father of lights, with whom there is no variation or shadow of turning." In other words, every good thing in life comes from God.

Therefore, since He is the one who gives you good things—your food, your health, your friends, the very air you breathe—and since He *wants* you to have His good gifts, doesn't it make sense to turn to Him often, to thank Him, and even to ask Him for more in the future?

Does that sound ungrateful—to ask for even more when God has already blessed you so abundantly? It might be, except for a second principle: *God loves to give.* When you ask for more and more blessing from the Father, you're inviting God to engage in one of His favorite activities.

You may find this easy or hard to believe, depending on your view of God. Maybe you see Him as a calculating cosmic accountant who ensures that all the good and bad in your life is ultimately balanced. Or maybe you see Him as a vengeful carrier of grudges who withholds blessing in proportion to all the sins you've committed since the day you were born. If you think either of these pictures describes God, you're not very likely to ask Him for blessing.

But God is exactly the opposite of those portrayals.

In Exodus 33:18, Moses asked God, "Please, show me Your glory." Scripture tells us twice in this context that God's reply to Moses was nothing less than a proclamation of His nature, which began, "The LORD, the LORD God, merciful and gracious, longsuffering, and abounding in goodness and truth" (Exodus 34:6–7).

He was saying, *When you have a need, I love to respond with mercy. When you are undeserving, I love to give graciously. When you try My patience, I am long, long, longsuffering. My goodness and truth overflow toward you and countless others. My love can breach even the barrier of your sin.*

Woven throughout the fabric of God's very Name are the shining golden bands of generous giving and blessing. This aspect of God's heart has never been more powerfully demonstrated than when He gave up the life of His own Son (see John 3:16).

As a father and a grandfather, I think I grasp just a little of the joy our heavenly Father experiences when He gives. If I'm resting at the beach with my grandsons and one of them "bothers" me by asking, "Granddad, would you build a sand castle with me?" or "Granddad, could you buy me an ice-cream cone?" I can't resist. I love them, and I love to give to them.

Yet God's generosity far outweighs that of the most gracious father—or grandfather—on earth.

WE'RE COMMANDED TO ASK

One Saturday night, one of our children asked if we could order a pizza. Before I knew it, all three kids were chiming in about how good an extra-cheese, thick-crust pizza would taste. I agreed. Now, if my children hadn't asked, they wouldn't have received the pizza they were craving. Was I willing to provide? Yes. But until asked, the reality of my willingness had not been engaged.

Could this be true of our Father in heaven?

If you are wondering whether our asking and receiving can be so tightly connected, James 4:2 leaves no doubt: "You do not have because you do not ask." All good things come from God, and God loves to give them. He bestows many blessings on every human—blessings such as life, possessions, a mind for thinking, and a heart for feeling. But God has chosen to require a step of initiative from us before He will release the fullness of His generosity.

We find the key to the truly abundant life in yet a third principle related to the Jabez prayer: *Some of God's greatest blessings are reserved for those who ask.*

Many people think that when you become a Christian, you are automatically added to God's full-blessing mailing list. But that isn't true. And until you believe that God is waiting for you to ask, you will miss out on one of the most remarkable, and at times supernatural, results of praying like Jabez.

How do we know this? In His Sermon on the Mount, Jesus revealed this underlying reality when He taught:

> "Ask, and it will be given to you; seek, and you will find; knock, and it will be opened to you. For everyone who asks receives, and he who seeks finds, and to him who knocks it will be opened."

> MATTHEW 7:7–8

Jesus is not merely offering a suggestion here. Read the passage again. The words *ask, seek,* and *knock* are written with imperative force—they are *commands!* In other words, to *not* ask would be to disobey God. Have you asked God to "give" to you recently?

Not only does Christ command us to ask, but in this passage He uses the present tense, which biblical scholars agree should be interpreted to mean "continue asking." The New Living Translation reads, "Keep on asking, and you will be given what you ask for." Christ commands us to continue asking until we receive.

So what are we commanded to ask *for?* Because of misconceptions about the Lord and His nature and ways, some believe that we can only ask for certain things, usually religious or spiritual in nature. These same people think that asking God for a gift is inappropriate—that one must earn something from God by being worthy, either through behavior or sacrifice.

Jesus anticipated that we would react to His boundless grace and generosity this way, so He gave us this helpful illustration:

> "What man is there among you who, if his son asks for bread, will give him a stone? Or if he asks for a fish, will he give him a serpent? If you then, being evil [when compared to God], know how to give good gifts to your children, how much more will your Father who is in heaven give good things to those who ask Him!"
>
> MATTHEW 7:9–11

Did you see the parallel Jesus makes between the words *gifts* and *good things?* He is teaching us to pray for gifts—for things we haven't earned. (In other passages Jesus teaches that He will reward everyone according to his works, but those rewards are based upon our actions and are never called gifts.)

The Father knows how to give you good things, *but you must ask!* If you used to pray for God's blessings or gifts of grace but for some reason have stopped, you undoubtedly have forfeited many a blessing. "You have not because you ask not." It's time to start praying again!

This is exactly what an amateur fisherman from Texas did. James was one of more than two thousand contestants vying for the largest amateur fishing tournament prize in the country—$100,000. And James's desire for the prize money was based on real need. His business earnings were at an all-time low, and his family was in danger of losing their home if God didn't provide for them soon. For six weeks, James had been prayerfully seeking God's blessing.

"How much more will your Father who is in heaven give good things to those who ask Him!"

So as he fished, he prayed.

After six hours, James reeled in a fighting 5.89-pound bass—the largest catch of the hour! But the tournament would not end until one o'clock the next afternoon. In every prior competition, the winning bass had weighed at least six pounds, so all the other fishermen knew they still had a chance.

The next morning, James was still in the lead and he prayed, *No matter what happens today, Lord, You are at work in my life, and that's all that matters.*

As the hours passed, he closely followed the radio broadcast of the tournament. And not without anxiety. But at the close of the contest, James was declared the champion! God had provided for his family in spectacular fashion.

Does God promise to provide in this same way for everyone? No. But there are many blessings God definitely *won't* give unless we ask. In this case, God's child requested a fish, and the Father gave him one.[2]

FIVE KINDS OF BLESSING

So what exactly do you have to do to receive blessings from praying the prayer of Jabez? This is where considerable misconceptions about the prayer have arisen. Some will tell you that other passages from the Old and New Testaments prove that unless you obey God you cannot receive any blessing from Him. They claim that all of God's blessings are tied to conditions of behavior.

Is this true? The Bible certainly doesn't teach that. In fact, the greatest blessing of all, the gift of salvation, is not given on the basis of any works that we may do!

If you were to study every instance in which the word or concept of "blessing" is used in the sixty-six books of the Bible, you would discover that there are at least five different types of blessings outlined in the Bible. Each of these five blessings is available through a particular avenue and based on a distinct set of conditions. Anytime you see God offer a gift or blessing in Scripture, it is important to ask which type of blessing it is.

The first of these is the *common good blessing*, which is given to everyone freely without any requirement. Jesus referred to this type of blessing when He said that God the Father "makes His sun rise on the evil and on the good, and sends rain on the just and on the unjust" (Matthew 5:45). This is a clear indication that God gives gifts even to those who are evil and wicked. This blessing is not determined by any behavior on your part; you get them just because you are alive. It's of interest that in this same sermon, Jesus instructs us to give gifts of kindness to those who are our enemies.

Second, the *conduct blessing* is given to those who meet a certain standard of behavior. If you behave a certain way, you will receive a certain blessing; if you don't, you won't receive the blessing. For example, God promised Israel, "Because you listen to these judgments, and keep and do them [the required behavior]...the LORD your God...will also bless the fruit of your womb and the fruit of your land, your grain and your new wine and your oil, the increase of your cattle and the offspring of your flock" (Deuteronomy 7:12–13). Some of the Beatitudes promise this type of blessing. For example, "Blessed are those who hunger and thirst for righteousness [the required behavior] for they shall be filled" (Matthew 5:6).

The third, the *conversion blessing*, is given to those who meet the requirement of belief. In the well-known verse John 3:16, Jesus says that salvation is a gift bestowed on those who believe: "For God so loved the world that He gave His only begotten Son, that whoever believes in Him should not perish but have everlasting life." In Ephesians 1:3, Paul wrote that God "has blessed us [those who place their trust in Christ alone] with every spiritual blessing in the heavenly places." The condition for receiving this blessing is very clear throughout the New Testament: You must place your faith in Jesus Christ for your salvation. The seriousness of altering the requirements for salvation, such as requiring works instead of faith, cannot be overstated.

The fourth, the *compensation blessing*, is given to everyone on the basis of their life conduct, and it is primarily given after death. Jesus once spoke to a wealthy crowd at a dinner party and said:

> "When you give a dinner or a supper, do not ask your friends, your brothers, your relatives, nor rich neighbors, lest they also invite you back, and you be repaid. But when you give a feast, invite the poor, the maimed, the lame, the blind. And you will be blessed, because they cannot repay you, *for you shall be repaid at the resurrection of the just.*"
>
> LUKE 14:12–14, EMPHASIS ADDED

The compensation blessing refers to the reward Christians will receive in heaven, after they die, for their conduct on earth. It's the same blessing Jesus promised us in Matthew 5:11–12: "Blessed are you when they revile and persecute you, and say all kinds of evil against you falsely for My sake. Rejoice and be exceedingly glad, for great is your reward in heaven." (See my book *A Life God Rewards*.)

Finally, there is the blessing for which Jabez prayed. The *compassion blessing* is given solely on the basis of God's character to those who ask. Time after time in the Gospels, you can read of Jesus healing scores of people just because they asked! It was rare that Jesus required a person to perform a certain act or change of behavior before being healed.

In the context of 1 Chronicles 4, we see no qualifications listed before or after Jabez's prayer—only the prayer itself. While a variety of conditions must be met in order to receive certain of the other four types of blessings, the Jabez blessing is different. What are the conditions in order to receive Jabez-type blessings? There's only one: *Ask.*

HOW MUCH BLESSING CAN YOU HANDLE?

Before speaking at a megachurch in Houston, I was standing off to the side, gathering my thoughts, when a woman quietly tapped me on the shoulder and said, "Dr. Wilkinson, I need help. I have committed a major sin."

I took a deep breath and asked, "How can I help you?"

"I sinned because of your book *The Prayer of Jabez*."

"You mean you sinned because of praying Jabez?"

"Yes. What should I do?"

I couldn't believe my ears. I had heard many strange things, but this was a first. She continued, "I couldn't handle it anymore. I prayed the prayer of Jabez every day for months, and the blessings kept coming and coming until I couldn't handle it anymore. So I sinned: I asked God to stop blessing me."

It happened again only a few days later. Our daughter was coming home from camp, and my wife and I were waiting for her bus in a grocery store parking lot. While we were standing there, a couple walked up and started sharing with us a whole string of amazing answers they had received to the Jabez prayer. Just then a man walked by, listened for a few moments, and interrupted. "Yup, the same thing happened to me. Finally, there was far too many blessings. I thought my heart would burst. So I asked the Lord to stop blessing me for a while, and I even stopped praying Jabez. But I have a question: Can I ask Him to start blessing me some more? Now I'm ready!"

Can you imagine that happening to you? Or are you still having trouble believing that God loves to bless His children extravagantly? Consider for a moment just how much God promised to bless the nation of Israel, as recorded in Deuteronomy:

"And all these blessings shall come upon you and overtake you [literally, you won't be able to escape the blessings!], because you obey the voice of the LORD your God [requirement for conduct blessing]:

"Blessed shall you be in the city, and blessed shall you be in the country.

"Blessed shall be the fruit of your body, the produce of your ground and the increase of your herds, the increase of your cattle and the offspring of your flocks.

"Blessed shall be your basket and your kneading bowl.

"Blessed shall you be when you come in. and blessed shall you be when you go out.

"The LORD will command the blessing on you in your storehouses and in all to which you set your hand.

"And the LORD will grant you plenty of goods, in the fruit of your body, in the increase of your livestock, and in the produce of your ground...

"The LORD will open to you His good treasure, the heavens, to give the rain to your land in its season, and to bless all the work of your hand [the blessings will fall on everything that you do]."

DEUTERONOMY 28:2–6, 8, 11–12

The God of the Old Testament is the same God of the New Testament. His great pleasure is to bless you so very much that you will have to ask Him to stop because you won't be able to handle even one more blessing! Don't allow yourself to miss the extravagant goodness of God who rejoices to answer those who ask. Read and cement 1 Corinthians 2:9 in your heart forever:

"Eye has not seen, nor ear heard, nor have entered into the heart of man the things which God has prepared for those who love Him."

If you find yourself saying, "I can't possibly imagine anyone being blessed so much that they have to ask for Him to stop," you are exactly right—the extent of His blessings have never been fully seen or heard or even thought of.

Why not stop now and invite Him to lovingly overwhelm you with the flood tide of His great blessing? He is just waiting to hear from you.

CHAPTER FOUR

THE PRAYER FOR
BLESSING:
LIVING IT OUT

*When we seek God's blessing as the ultimate value in life,
we are throwing ourselves entirely into the river of His will
and power and purposes for us. All our other needs
become secondary to what we really want—which is to
become wholly immersed in what God is trying to do in us,
through us, and around us for His glory.[1]*

THE PRAYER OF JABEZ

I remember the first reporter who called me for an
interview about *The Prayer of Jabez.* She had asked me
many questions and we were about to wrap it up when I
said to her, "Now I have a question for you: Will you pray
the prayer of Jabez for thirty days and then write an article
about what happens? If nothing happens, then say so. But

if something does, would you write about it?"

"No," she said, "I'm not going to do that."

"Why not?" I asked.

"I'll tell you what," she said, searching for a fair compromise, "I'm going to *meditate* on the prayer of Jabez."

"That's nice," I said, "but that's not going to work."

"Why not?"

"Because the prayer of Jabez is a *prayer*. It's part of a conversation between you and another Person—a Person to whom you make requests and who is able to grant your requests."

In the end she steadfastly refused. She was willing to learn *about* the Bible, but she didn't want to make it part of her life.

So far we have examined a lot of information—valuable information—*about* praying for blessing. Now it's time to go beyond mere knowledge into action. The Jabez prayer for blessing won't do you or me one bit of good unless we actually pray it.

So how can we go about praying this prayer most effectively? How can we learn to live more in keeping with the God who loves to give?

NEW ATTITUDES ABOUT BLESSINGS

The first practical guideline is simply this: *Pray for God's blessing. Every day.* Don't let a day go by when you might miss out on a heavenly gift just because you didn't ask. Start today.

The second guideline will help you develop a heart like Jabez's: *Frequently thank God for His many blessings.* In a journal, keep a running list of God's expressions of His goodness toward you, whether they've come in response to prayer, or unsolicited out of His overflowing generosity. Try this for a few weeks. Let your heart sing with David's, "Bless the LORD, O my soul, and forget not all His benefits" (Psalm 103:2). Gradually, your heart will fill with gratitude as you learn to reinterpret "coincidences" you previously overlooked. Instead of thinking dismissively, *Well, that was a nice surprise,* you'll begin to rejoice and say to others, "Wait until I tell you what God has done for me!"

Third, *enjoy God's blessings.* Paul wrote to the young pastor Timothy about our God "who gives us richly all things to enjoy" (1 Timothy 6:17). As we live in faith toward God, He wants us to have a good time with His gifts.

But, God, you might say, *I don't deserve this.*

You're right, He responds, *you don't. It's a gift. Enjoy it!*

A man once told me about the abundance of God's blessing in his life. "He keeps blessing and blessing. It's amazing. But it's all going to change."

That surprised me. "What do you mean, 'It's all going to change'?"

"One day," he said, "the other shoe's going to fall. You can only have so many good things before it has to equal out, and the bad has to come."

I'm not sure where he got that idea, but it wasn't from God. This man was restricting himself from enjoying God's blessing. And God's heart.

CONDUITS OF BLESSING

At the same time, we would be terribly mistaken if we kept all of God's gracious gifts to ourselves. The fourth practical guideline for praying for blessing is this: *Share your blessings with others.*

Paul encourages those who are blessed with much to "be rich in good works, ready to give, willing to share" (1 Timothy 6:18). This is where the prayer for blessing connects most strongly with Jabez's request for territory, which we will study in greater depth in later chapters. This is also the main theme of my book *The Dream Giver.* Yes, God wants you to enjoy His blessings, but He also wants you to use them to make a difference in the world around you. When God gives you something, share it!

As I write so much during the day, I particularly enjoy a very special pen that a friend gave to me—a Mont Blanc pen. It's my favorite writing utensil, and there's an amazing story behind it.

Years ago, before *The Prayer of Jabez* was published, Darlene Marie and I experienced an unexpected financial outpouring of God's blessing, and we felt that He wanted us to share some of it somehow with another person as a gesture of thanks to God. We sought His guidance, but weeks went by and neither of us had any clear ideas.

Then our refrigerator broke.

As we pulled into the appliance store parking lot, Darlene Marie and I were pondering aloud where God might want us to direct His gift. Still we had no clue. We went into the store and the salesman—a man from Africa—was very helpful as we made our selection. We accepted the store's offer of zero-interest-for-a-year financing, and I pulled out my pen to sign the contract.

The salesman's eyes widened. "That's a Mont Blanc pen!" he said.

"Yes, sir," I replied. "This is my favorite pen."

Now, I'll be honest. Inwardly I cringed, because one of the few material things in life in which I take particular pleasure is my Mont Blanc pen. I could already feel myself defending against the inevitable.

Sure enough, the salesman said, in a quiet, reminiscing sort of way, "One of my lifelong goals, before I go back to Africa, is to own a Mont Blanc pen."

Lord, no! I shouted inside. *Not my pen. Let me give him money!*

I glanced over at Darlene Marie. She was trying not to laugh.

But God's message was clear. Shaking my head in amazement, I said, "Sir, I've been carrying around somebody else's pen for a long time, and I've enjoyed it. But the owner just alerted me that He'd like you to have it. His name is the Lord God, and here is His gift to you. Enjoy it!"

God wants you to enjoy His blessings—and to use them to make a difference in the world around you.

Well, the story doesn't end there. God had used the pen incident to teach me a valuable lesson—that God often asks for the very thing we hold on to too tightly—and I shared the story some time later at my friend Dr. David Jeremiah's church in San Diego, California. A year later I was attending the annual convention of the Christian Booksellers of America when one day, in a crowd of thousands, someone called my name. I turned to see Tim LaHaye, coauthor of the Left Behind series, calling to me.

He said, "David sent me a tape of your sermon—the one where you told the story about the pen."

"Oh, yes," I said. "That was a long time ago."

Then he said, "As I was listening to your sermon, guess what God conveyed to me?" He reached into his pocket. "He said, *Give Bruce your Mont Blanc pen.*" And he handed me his pen—the one that I now have, even to this day!

ANTICIPATE THE POTENTIAL!

What can you expect when you pray faithfully for God's bountiful blessing? You can expect exactly what He has promised: *bountiful blessing.* God granted Jabez's request because this is a prayer He wants to answer.

None of us can predict what form God's gifts will take. They may come in material form, or they may be spiritual or relational. Or something else entirely. But they will be good because they come from the King of givers.

Carol and her husband started a family-owned engineering firm, but they struggled financially from day one. For years they prayed together regularly, "Lord, we want to do Your will." And they puzzled over their lack of visible success.

Then they learned about the prayer of Jabez and incorporated it into their daily prayer times, eagerly anticipating the blessings He had in store.

And their financial situation got worse.

Carol became so frustrated that she asked God to explain His silence. "Father, why do You bless others and ignore us? Are we doing something wrong?"

The Lord answered by opening their understanding. The couple came to realize that they had been restricting their view of God's blessing to the material, but that there was so much more He wanted them to have.

At first glance, the prayer of Jabez had seemed to be all about *them,* but they suddenly knew that it was all about *Him.* His will, His wisdom, His choice of blessings, His timing.

Remember, when Jabez prayed for God's blessing, he didn't specify what he wanted the blessing to be, but he instead relied on the Lord's wisdom to select the blessing and bestow it at the most opportune time.

And so, though the couple continued to struggle with their finances, they began experiencing God's abundant *spiritual* blessing as their faith in His provision was stretched and strengthened. This couple had previously thought of the prayer for blessing as a "magic bullet" that would take care of their outward problems. But God addressed a higher priority first—their spiritual maturity—which was by far the greater blessing in the grand scope of life.[2]

TOO MUCH BLESSING?

We have such a hard time believing that life can be so abundant. *Yet that's the way God meant it to be.* We love and serve an infinite God who gives and gives and who delights in our joy. Sometimes the blessings come piled on top of blessings. Other times they arrive in the midst of difficult trials that build maturity and inner strength. In any event, if you open your heart to God, He will fill it to overflowing.

And what will God do with your surplus blessing? He will use you as a source of blessing for *others*. We are to imitate His generosity all the time, even when we don't have much (see 2 Corinthians 8:1–4); but how much more could you give if your life were filled to overflowing?

Why does God choose to use us to bless others? Couldn't He just as easily bless these people directly? Certainly. But part of His strategy for growing us to spiritual maturity is to entrust us with extra and then invite us to share with others.

Sharing is a learned skill, and when God showers down more blessing than we need for ourselves, He's providing us with a learning opportunity.

In fact, Jesus put blessing that is shared into a special category of its own: "It is more blessed to give than to receive" (Acts 20:35). Is it wrong to receive? No, it's fine, and some of us need to receive more willingly. But *even more blessed* is the act of giving.

God may even bless you so much that you can't handle it, to the point that you *have* to share with others. In my experience, this special blessing only comes to those who really want it and who pray faithfully for months and sometimes years.

Keep praying fervently to God, "Bless me a lot. Pour out Your abundant blessings on me." Then when He knows you're ready, He'll start bringing to you people with great needs or who represent great causes, and you will discover that He has changed your heart so that you greatly desire to give. You'll go to bed at night and realize that the most significant activity of your day was giving, not getting.

God loves to bless us, but He loves even more watching His children imitate their Father by reaching out and blessing others.

The Honor of Being Asked

These lessons were reinforced for me during one of the most unexpected and pivotal experiences of my life. My whole family was sitting around our den talking when, during a quiet moment in the conversation, my son, David, leaned forward and asked, "Dad, would you do something for me?"

"Sure, Dave," I said, "I'll be glad to. What do you have in mind?"

"Dad," he said, "I want you to bless me."

That caught me by surprise, "Sure, Son, of course. I bless you."

He shook his head. "No, Dad. I mean *really* bless me."

With that, David quietly stood up, walked across to where I was seated, and knelt at my feet. He looked up at me. "Please, Dad, I really want your blessing." Then he lowered his head.

I've rarely felt more deeply touched or honored in my life.

Emotion welled up as I placed my hands on his shoulders and poured out my deepest heart to bless our son with everything in me. I blessed and I blessed. I prayed about our dreams for him and the gifts and talents God had given him. I thanked God for his past and I prayed for his future.

I gave until there was nothing left to give.

Then, without a word, David stood and walked back to his seat.

As David sat down, the Lord whispered to me, *Now you know how I feel when you come to Me, when you kneel before My throne and ask Me to bless you!*

Why would we knowingly deprive such a Father of the honor He receives when we ask? Or the pleasure He derives from answering? Never again let a day pass without looking into His face and saying, "Oh, God, please bless me indeed."

PART II

INFLUENCE FOR GOD

And Jabez called on the God of Israel saying,
"Oh, that You would bless me indeed,
and enlarge my territory,
that Your hand would be with me,
and that You would keep me from evil,
that I may not cause pain!"
So God granted him what he requested.

People Who Prayed

RENEWAL SCORES
IN RWANDA

by Don Brenneman

The history of Rwanda is filled with tragedy. In 1994, in this African country not much bigger than Rhode Island, 800,000 nationals were massacred in a tribal civil war. From the government to the churches, trust was destroyed on every level. Unity seemed impossible.

But Archbishop Kolini, the head of the Anglican Church in Rwanda, had faith that God could use a simple soccer game to bring healing to his country.

That's where I came in. I'm the Director of Development for the Sports Outreach Institute (SOI), a Christian agency that builds and equips sports ministries around the world. When Archbishop Kolini asked our ministry to help him bring down the walls of hatred in Rwanda, we seized the opportunity and began two prayer-filled years of preparation for the Rwandan Football Crusade.

It was a God-sized task. In order for the effort to impact

the whole nation, the American team—the Charlotte Eagles—would need to play in the capital city's national stadium. The government, the business community, churches, and sports federations would all need to work together. Many said it could never happen.

At first the government and the Rwandan Football Federation resisted the crusade. But when Archbishop Kolini rallied the churches of Rwanda, both institutions eventually gave their consent and, later, their enthusiastic support. This was among the first of countless miracles.

The history-making event was only two months away when my pastor preached on the prayer of Jabez. And so I began praying daily for, among other things, enlarged territory for SOI and for the Rwandan pastors.

Finally, the day of the event arrived and, for the first time in history, an American soccer team played on Rwandan soil. Three games were scheduled over four days. The second and third were played in the national stadium, which not long before had been surrounded by barbed wire and occupied by United Nations peacekeepers.

Tens of thousands of people attended the matches, sometimes braving torrential rain. At the third match we were honored to host the president of Rwanda, several of his Cabinet members, and the American ambassador.

During each game's halftime, the American athletes presented the message of hope in Christ, and afterward they stayed to talk further with the crowds. Many nationals heard the name of Jesus for the first time, and thousands made life-changing commitments.

But the impact of this event extended far beyond the stadiums. The last two matches, complete with halftime presentations, were broadcast live by radio to an estimated *eight million listeners* throughout Rwanda and neighboring nations.

And distrustful Rwandans took one giant step toward long-term reconciliation.

In the words of one team member, "The nation of Rwanda has been changed forever."

CHAPTER FIVE

THE PRAYER FOR
TERRITORY:
A CLOSER LOOK

Soon, Ordinary was walking away from the comfortable
center of Familiar, where almost every Nobody lived.
He was heading toward the Border, where almost no Nobodies
ever went. Ordinary had never dared to walk this way before.
But, like every Nobody, he knew that the farther you walked
from the center of Familiar, the less familiar things became.
He also knew that most Nobodies who tried to leave the
Comfort Zone of Familiar became so uncomfortable,
they turned around and went home.[1]

THE DREAM GIVER

*S*ometimes the first time is the most vivid. It was 1974,
during our first year in Portland, Oregon, where I was
teaching college and graduate school. Darlene Marie and I

were still trying to understand how this Jabez prayer worked, so we decided to conduct a test—we would pray for expanded territory in a very specific manner.

We talked it over, then asked the Lord to send us people to be discipled without our saying a word to anyone. Darlene Marie began to pray that God would expand her territory by sending her three college girls to be discipled or mentored. I started to pray that God would send the student body president to walk into my office and ask, "Will you meet with me each week to disciple me?"

Our excitement ran high the first few days we prayed. But then weeks went by and nothing happened. We started to lose hope that God would answer this type of prayer for specific territory.

After the semester ended, I flew to Boise, Idaho, to speak at a local church. I remember lying in bed that night and asking the Lord why He wouldn't answer our prayers. I found out later that back at home Darlene Marie was asking the same question.

The next evening, when I got up to speak, I couldn't believe my eyes: The student body president I had been praying for was sitting in the audience—hundreds of miles away from the college!

After the service about twenty of us, including this young man, gathered at a nearby pizza shop. I was tempted to ask him then and there if he would like to meet on a regular basis, but that would have ruined the test. Either God would answer my prayer or He wouldn't.

The student body president was sitting at the far end of four tables that had been pushed together. All of a sudden, in the middle of pepperoni and laughter, the young man stood up and in an emotionally charged outburst said, "Professor

Wilkinson, will you disciple me when we get back to college?"

There was stunned silence around the tables. Finally, I stammered, "Why are you asking me this now?"

Then tears filled his eyes and the young man said, "From the first day I sat in your class, I knew I was supposed to meet with you on a weekly basis, but I was too scared to ask. Tonight, I knew that God had given me one more chance, and I wasn't going to blow it again!"

I flew back on flight number Cloud 9, astonished at how dramatically God had answered my prayer for more territory. As it turned out, Darlene Marie was thrilled as well, because each day I was gone, a different young woman from the college had called and asked to be discipled by her. Three students, just as she had prayed.

JABEZ'S SECOND REQUEST

In these next few chapters, we will examine in greater depth what Jabez meant by the second part of his prayer: "Enlarge my territory." At the outset we must observe that Jabez was most likely praying for an area of land. Jabez was apparently either a farmer or a herdsman; his livelihood required a certain area of fertile fields or pastureland. In the simplest of terms, Jabez was asking God to enlarge the land that he owned, thereby increasing the size of his business.

Also, we see that Jabez asked God to "enlarge" his territory. *Enlarge* means "to abundantly increase." The Hebrew word implies not just a little growth, but a huge expansion. It's the same word translated as "multiply" in Genesis 1:28, in which God commanded Adam and Eve, "Be fruitful and multiply; fill the earth"—their assignment was to increase mankind from just two people to an earthful. Jabez wasn't seeking a little blessing or just a little more land—he was asking for a vast abundance!

Recently, my chief operating officer and I were investigating how we might expand Dream for Africa to the southern African nation of Zambia. Meetings were conducted with Zambia's department of education, the department of agriculture, church leaders, and the country's president. At every turn, the nation's leaders responded with enthusiasm to our initiatives involving hunger, orphans, poverty, and AIDS. But we were still uncertain where the greatest need lay.

On the evening before we met with the president, a bishop of the Anglican Church, who was helping to coordinate these meetings, came to me and said he felt that we needed the Lord to break through in a major way with the president the next morning. I felt burdened by the large number of orphans we had seen in the nation and began praying that God would expand our territory to Zambia in a vast way and that the president would be the vehicle of His answer. I asked the Lord to lead the president the next morning to give us twenty-five thousand acres for our orphan initiative.

Jabez was asking for a vast abundance!

Even though I've met with many heads of state, one never can predict what will happen in the first meeting. We were slotted for twenty minutes with the Zambian president, but the meeting lasted an hour and a half. After reviewing our four major initiatives, I asked the president which one of them he would be most interested in for his nation. Instantly he indicated our African Dream Villages for orphans. He explained that his nation of ten million people currently had more than 600,000 orphans, with estimates reaching one million by the year 2010.

Our African Dream Village initiative seeks to provide nurturing homes (with mothers and fathers), schools of excellence, and training in business and entrepreneurial skills for 5 percent of the orphans in a nation. Unfortunately, in many locations throughout Africa, AIDS and tuberculosis have decimated the villages and extended family structure, leaving untold thousands of households headed by orphaned children. These are our burden—the vulnerable children that have proven to be beyond the capabilities of church, society, and government.

I told the president that Dream for Africa's vision was to care for 5 percent, or fifty thousand, of his country's orphans—all in private homes in a family atmosphere. "But it will take a massive piece of property to achieve this," I explained, "along with access to a year-round river for growing all the food for the families as well as earning income from agricultural exports. If this can be done, I believe that thousands of African, American, European, Asian, and Australian volunteers will come to Zambia and help us build hundreds of homes and schools in the next three years."

After further discussion, the president said, "Zambia will give Dream for Africa ten thousand hectares for our first African Dream Villages—and more if you need them for fifty thousand orphans!"

That night as I was praying, I began thanking the Lord for those ten thousand hectares—and then remembered that a hectare is the equivalent of two and a half acres! In a single meeting, God had expanded our territory by twenty-five thousand acres. His heart breaks for Africa's orphans, and I

believe He will expand anyone's territory if they seek the
welfare of those in severe need.

IN EVERY DIRECTION

Enlarge my territory. I encourage you to pray this for all of your
God-honoring pursuits. Much of what God wants us to do
involves the expansion of not only literal territory, but
influence as well. He wants to use you and the talents and
skills He has entrusted to you to touch more and more of the
people of the world.

Think of your life territory as a box with different sides.
One side of the territory represents your family, another your
work, another your ministry, another your personal
relationships, and so on. In a very real sense, God desires to
increase your influence for Him in each and every one of
these areas. As I have shared at greater length in *The Dream
Giver,* when you discover the Big Dream for which you were
born, you'll find that it somehow involves helping other
people in more and more significant ways.

That brings me to the first of four clarifying distinctives
of the prayer for territory: *The prayer is not focused only on gaining
property, but on expanding ministry (service).*

In fact, sometimes God pushes our efforts solely in the
direction of ministry to others, even when we have different
plans. That's what happened to John Waller and his Christian
band, According to John (A2J).

The band was riding a wave of financial success. They had
toured nationally and their CDs were selling well. But then
their record label went bankrupt and closed its doors. The
band attempted its own independent recording project, but it

flopped. They went to Nashville and auditioned for several recording labels, but found no takers.

Around this time, John's pastor began a sermon series based on the prayer of Jabez, which challenged John to rethink his objectives.

And so he prayed, *Okay, Lord, You have my attention. If You don't expand our ministry, it just isn't going to happen. Let Your will be done.*

One night John was preparing to lead worship for a Wednesday-night youth service, and he decided to teach the prayer of Jabez to the kids through a song. And so he wrote "The Song of Jabez." The teens loved it.

Word got out, and A2J was asked to play the song for the church board of directors. One of the board members responded enthusiastically, "You need to record that song!" And he offered to put up the money for the recording.

"There's just one stipulation," the chairman added. "You have to give the song away."

The band recorded the song and began distributing it on CDs and via their website. They encouraged people to make copies and pass them around.

Somehow a copy found its way to Focus on the Family headquarters, and Dr. Dobson played it on one of his broadcasts, making the song available to callers upon request.

With this national attention, "The Song of Jabez" quickly became the number three inspirational single in the nation. There's no way of knowing how many millions of people have been encouraged and guided by its message.

God had used hardship to help the band take their focus off outward indications of success. Fame and financial achievement are not wrong in themselves; God simply had something different in mind for John and his friends. Now their goal is to be contagious for Christ—to help set hearts on fire for God.[2]

GOD'S TERRITORY OR MINE?

The story of these musicians illustrates a second distinction of the prayer for territory: *The choice of new territory is usually not self-initiated, but God-directed.*

It's good to make plans, and it's fine to ask God to bless your plans. But the Jabez prayer for more territory is similar to asking for more blessing in that it doesn't specify where or when or how, but instead asks God to take us past our limited horizons: *I want* You *to guide my expanding influence.*

While still leading WorldTeach, I asked Darlene Marie to join with me in praying that God would open the doors to meet with the presidents of Kenya and Zambia during an upcoming trip to Africa. She was surprised because, until that time, I had never expressed any interest in such meetings. When she asked about it, I told her that I was unsure as to the purpose, but I felt that the Lord wanted to enlarge our territory in this direction.

In the middle of a week of training a thousand leaders how to respond to the AIDS crisis, I was asked to meet with the president of Kenya. During the trip to the palace, I questioned the Lord as to His purpose, but no answer surfaced. Heaven remained silent.

President Moi proved to be a gracious host, and during the meeting I asked him the question: "You are president of one of the greatest nations in Africa. Is there anything that weighs on you or keeps you awake at night, where I could perhaps be of some small assistance?"

His face softened as he responded, "People come here all the time to ask me to do something for *them*. You are asking if you could help *me*!"

After a few moments, President Moi said something I never expected. "Thousands of my people are dying from AIDS. I wish I had a Hollywood movie—a drama—that would take the many misconceptions about HIV/AIDS and bring about a major behavioral change and save my nation." Then he just looked at me, and my heart pounded as I found myself realizing that this was the very reason the Lord had burdened me to meet with him.

I committed to produce such a movie, and the result was a powerful two-hour drama about a young Zulu boy who, when his parents die of AIDS, moves to Sowetto and tries to find his way while living under a bridge. I formed a film production company, which produced the internationally award-winning motion picture *Beat the Drum*. The film is having a profound impact across Africa. (For more information on the film, visit www.dreamforafrica.com.)

When you pray, "Dear Lord, please enlarge my territory for You—please let me do much more for You," there's no telling how the Lord might choose to fulfill your request!

This brings us to a third distinctive: *The prayer for territory is not focused on your comfort, but on change.* Whenever you ask for "more," you really are asking God to take you beyond where you have ever been before—into the unknown and unpredictable. God has an exciting adventure waiting for you, and it will involve some risks. But as you grow to know personally the God who urges you to exercise greater influence for Him, you'll soon learn that He will never abandon you.

And as you accept the changes, you will discover the

fourth distinctive of the prayer for territory: *God's territory for you is not limited, but limitless.* After praying this way for three decades and watching thousands of people experience God's answers, one thing is clear to me—there's no limit to how much God may increase your territory.

Although you may feel overwhelmed at first, just remember that God will never expand your territory beyond where He knows the two of you can achieve His goals. On the other hand, however, just imagine a lifetime of experiencing the wonder and adventure of His answers to your prayers.

WHO IS RESPONSIBLE?

Sometimes people are reluctant to do more for God. They feel stretched beyond their limits as it is. But anyone willing to break through their fears will discover that life is best and most satisfying when we're living God's adventure.

I've recognized three primary misconceptions that get in the way of our living to our highest potential.

TERRITORY MISCONCEPTION #1:
God is responsible for the results; I'm not.

You might think that I'm affirming an opposite and equally erroneous misconception—namely, that when you step out in faith *you* have full responsibility for the results. That's not what I'm saying. Rather, God commands you to *share* full responsibility with Him.

If you're waiting passively for God to do all the work in enlarging your territory, you are overlooking the active role He has assigned you. When you realize and embrace your share of the responsibility for increasing fruitfulness in your life, you will discover new motivation to pray the prayer of Jabez!

The truth is, God will hold you accountable for your life's productivity, just as Jesus taught His disciples. He explained to them that He would soon be leaving, and He promised to return at an undisclosed time. The question naturally arose in their minds, *What are we supposed to do while You're gone?* Jesus answered them with a parable told in Luke 19:11–27.

The story tells of a nobleman—representing Jesus Himself—who is about to depart to claim a faraway kingdom, then later return. He calls together ten of his servants and entrusts each of them with one mina, which represents about three years' wages. He instructs them, "Put this money to work. Do business till I return."

Upon his return, the nobleman is eager to learn how his investments have fared, so he gathers the ten servants. The first man steps forward and says, "Master, your mina has earned ten minas," to which the nobleman responds, "Well done, good servant; because you were faithful in a very little, you will have authority over ten cities."

The second servant says, "Master, your mina has earned five minas." The nobleman answers, "You shall be over five cities."

Then the third man comes forward and unwraps his mina from the handkerchief where he has been keeping it. He hands the mina back to the nobleman, saying, "Master, your money has been safe all this time." He had hidden it away, fearful of his master's displeasure should he lose it. At least, that was his excuse.

The man could hardly have displeased his master more. He had directly disobeyed the nobleman's instructions to invest the money. With great displeasure, the nobleman takes the man's mina and gives it to the servant who has ten—the one who has proven most productive.

Each man had been given the same opportunity, and the master responded with approval and honor in keeping with the results of each man's performance. What each man received was earned by his diligent, hard work in maximizing what the nobleman had entrusted to him.

As Jesus taught, "Everyone to whom much is given, from him much will be required" (Luke 12:48). What has Jesus given us to invest? He's entrusted each of us with a valuable treasure—a lifetime of nearly unlimited opportunity. And He's instructed us, *Multiply your life for Me. When I come back, I will ask you what you did with it.*

Granted, we cannot do anything of eternal value without God. That's why Jesus promises to be with us (see Matthew 28:20) and to provide us power and wisdom through His Spirit (see Acts 1:8; John 14:26). But He also assigns us to take an active role: *You do business till I come.* To be more productive, ask for more territory!

ARE NUMBERS SPIRITUAL?

Some people object to the prayer for territory on the grounds that God is interested in quality, not quantity.

TERRITORY MISCONCEPTION # 2:
God is interested in spiritual things, not in numbers.

But consider carefully. Jesus said, "You did not choose Me, but I chose you and appointed you that you should go and bear fruit, and that your fruit should remain" (John 15:16). By *fruit,* Jesus was referring not only to the good things we do for Him, but to the people whom we help come into a closer relationship with Him.

Okay, Lord. But how much fruit do you want?

"By this My Father is glorified, that you bear *much* fruit" (John 15:8, emphasis added).

The truth is, the Lord desires that your life produce both quality *and* quantity. Quantity counts! Therefore, it's thoroughly biblical to pray, *Lord, enlarge my territory greatly! Let me do a lot for you!* Take what God has entrusted to you and multiply it ten times for Him, for in this way God's reputation is advanced.

WHAT ABOUT FEAR?

This brings me to yet another problematic viewpoint. I'll admit, this one stopped me for years. Anytime God brought me to the edge of my comfort zone and invited me to step over into "the wild," I would think, *I don't know what might be out there. I could get hurt. Or fail.* My line of reasoning went like this: *I feel afraid. Therefore, this must not be God's will.*

And so I remained safe. And my borders stayed exactly where they had been before.

TERRITORY MISCONCEPTION #3:
If I'm doing God's will, I won't be afraid.

The truth is, sometimes you *will* be afraid. But the Lord will be with you, no matter what you're facing.

After the Israelites had wandered in the wilderness for

forty years, Moses appointed Joshua as his successor, to lead the nation into and conquer the Promised Land. Joshua had watched for four decades as a failed, faithless generation dwindled away, and he must have thought many times, *How can I be sure Israel will do any better under my leadership?*

But when the time came, God told Joshua, "Be strong and of good courage; do not be afraid, nor be dismayed, for the LORD your God is with you wherever you go" (Joshua 1:9). Clearly, Joshua had known fear. And yet he obeyed in spite of his fear, leading Israel into one of the most glorious, faith-filled periods in the nation's history.

It's natural to feel fear when faced with the unknown, especially when the obstacles look bigger than ourselves. This is an issue I tried to clarify in *The Dream Giver:*

> In my experience, God rarely makes our fear disappear. Instead, He asks us to be strong and take courage. What is courage? Not the absence of fear; rather, it's choosing to act in spite of the fear. You could say that without fear, you can't have genuine courage.[3]

Those who are afraid and obey anyway are to be admired and honored.

God may ask you to face potential embarrassment or rejection as you do His work in the new territory He gives you. He may even give you a task at which you could fail. Some of the "dangers" confronting you will exist only in your imagination; on the other hand, you could be called on to risk your life. Whatever the situation, whatever the odds— even when you're paralyzed with terror—God will never leave you.

WILL YOU ANSWER THE CALL?

Perhaps you are still under the illusion that you are unworthy or incapable of handling more territory and, therefore, have no business asking. Nothing could be further from the truth. Ask and the Lord will decide how best to answer.

A few years ago, I was in Los Angeles to speak to hundreds of Hollywood directors, producers, writers, and other talent who wanted to hear for themselves how a little book on prayer could outsell Stephen King, John Grisham, and the other popular authors of our day. This was a diverse audience of Christians, Jews, agnostics, atheists, confirmed secularists, New Age adherents, occultists, and everything in between!

"I've never stood before a more creative group of people in my life," I said to the assembly. "You have entertained my family, made us laugh, made us cry, and inspired us to become all we can be. You have enriched our lives. Thank you."

Then I paused and smiled. It was obvious they weren't expecting a "religious" writer to affirm them. I continued, "And to be honest, you have also produced some material that didn't help anyone, except perhaps those who profited by its production." Everyone laughed. No one disagreed. This was Hollywood.

I went on to talk about the four parts of the prayer of Jabez, and I mentioned that God nearly always answered this part of the prayer. I explained that, in fact, expanded borders (God's letting us do more for Him) was the subject of more than three-fourths of all the letters I had been receiving from people who had read the book—people who were stunned and thrilled by how dramatically the Lord had answered their prayers for more territory.

It was obvious that many in the crowd were having

Just pray and watch for whom God will send into your path.

difficulty believing that God would answer such a prayer, so I asked them, "With a show of hands, how many of you have been in at least one situation where you knew, without a doubt, that God wanted you to go and help someone in need—but, for one reason or another, you didn't?"

Nearly every hand shot up.

I said, "Now maybe you can understand why when someone prays, 'Please God, send me to someone who needs You; let me be Your hands and feet,' God almost always provides an amazing answer. At any given time, millions of people are praying to Him for help, but so few people are willing to go and be that help."

If you are willing to raise your voice and say, "Here I am, please send me," you never have to wonder whether God answers the prayer of Jabez. Just pray and watch for whom God will send into your path.

WILL GOD ALWAYS ANSWER THIS PRAYER?

Will God always expand my territory if I ask Him to? I'm a little bit reluctant to answer this question, but I feel it's an important one.

There are two basic approaches to praying for enlarged territory. The most common is to ask God to enlarge your territory, then prepare yourself for His answers. The other approach is to pray for more territory, then turn around and engage someone on the spot because whoever is nearby may well be within your new territory.

My favorite way to open a conversation is to ask the other person a very simple question: "What can I do for you?" Almost without fail, the person responds, "Um...nothing." But time after time, I have found that a need—new territory—exists just beneath the surface. That is, until my encounter with a television executive.

The plane was full. I was tired and didn't want to talk to anyone. The woman seated next to me didn't seem to want to talk either, so we kept to ourselves. When dinner was served, I finally turned to the woman and asked my "Jabez question."

"What can I do for you?" I asked.

"What? Nothing, of course."

We talked for a few moments, then I asked her a second time.

"What can I do for you?"

"What are you talking about?" she protested. "You can't do *anything* for me."

Over dessert I took a deep breath and asked the question for a third time (I've never had to ask more than twice, before or since). This time I received a very sharp answer. She wanted nothing to do with my offer of help.

I blushed, as you probably would have. After hundreds of times of asking that question of people in countries all over the world, I had finally encountered a situation in which it seemed God would not answer my prayer for more territory.

My heart sank. Disappointment. Discouragement. Embarrassment. I prayed to the Lord, *Is this the first time You are going to say no?* If the Lord wanted to say no, that was fine with me. After all, who wants to go where the Lord isn't leading? Unfortunately, I couldn't find any peace about ending the conversation.

So with all the courage I could muster, I turned to the

woman and said, "Please don't be offended, but you aren't telling the truth."

She nearly exploded. "How on earth did you know? How *could* you know?"

I told her I didn't know anything about her situation but sensed that I could serve her in some way.

She looked down and said, "I'm feeling terrible and wonderful at the same time. I've almost got him." She told me she was the head of a television network and was returning from a board meeting with a national media company. She and another executive had been secretly meeting at these board meetings for the past two years and had been having an affair. "I've almost got him away from his wife and children," she said.

I prayed for wisdom and replied, "How does God feel about your destroying a marriage and family?"

She looked down and was quiet for a moment. "I don't think He is in favor of it."

"Maybe that's why I'm here," I said. "Maybe that's how I can help you."

For the next two hours, we had a very sensitive but straightforward conversation. We landed at the airport, but she still hadn't made the break. I pleaded for the hand of God to intervene, and I asked if she would be open to having a cup of coffee on the concourse before she caught her connecting flight. She faltered but said yes. Thankfully, the Lord did intervene and before I headed for the baggage claim, she wept in repentance. She agreed to call the man and apologize and end the affair and committed to resigning from the board of directors so that she wouldn't see him again.

As I sat down in the underground tram in the airport, I smiled. The Lord reigns and He loves to answer the heartfelt request, *Oh God, please send me.*

THE REST OF THIS CHAPTER WASN'T SUPPOSED TO BE IN THE BOOK

I was working on this chapter while on a flight to Los Angeles, where I was to speak at Biola University. As I finished up the previous paragraph (the remainder of this chapter was not in the original manuscript), I turned to the window and prayed, *Lord, would you validate the prayer of Jabez for me once again? Would you make it extra clear? I'm not going to say a word to the person next to me, but would you expand my territory to include him?*

Minutes later, the man sitting next to me asked if I was a priest.

"Why do you ask?" I said.

He said, "Well, I've been reading over your shoulder as you were marking up the book. It's really interesting!"

I smiled. "Well, I guess you could call me a priest."

"I knew it—God sent you!"

He then started weeping uncontrollably. The man had numerous tattoos and rings. He was on his way to the Hollywood Bowl, where he was in charge of a massive rock concert the next day. He said he didn't know what he was going to do; he had been drinking so much that the stewardess said she wouldn't give him another bottle for a while. His best friend had died the day before, and he was desperate for answers about eternity and about where his friend might be.

We had an incredible conversation. And once again I learned that God granted not only Jabez what he requested, but He does so for all who ask with the heart of Jabez, "Expand my territory!"

CHAPTER SIX

THE PRAYER FOR
TERRITORY:
GOING DEEPER

I can count as many scars as successes on the journey
to my Dream. The way of the Dreamer is difficult—
but anything less is hardly living at all!
In fact, I've discovered that it's the only way you and I can find
true fulfillment and become all that God created us to be.[1]

THE DREAM GIVER

W hat image comes to mind when you picture Moses?
Many of us envision Charlton Heston standing
majestically at the edge of a rugged cliff, his white-bearded
visage stern and commanding, his long robes billowing, his
strong arms holding aloft the huge stone tablets.

Indeed, this might describe Moses at some point during
the final decades of his 120 years. But if we were to rewind the

film a bit to when Moses was a mere eighty, we see a quite
different man—a man cowering from the territory God had
commanded him to take, unwilling to leave the familiar life of
a desert sheepherder.

You may recall that during his first forty years Moses was
raised as royalty among the influential elite of the world
power Egypt. Then, after a violently misguided attempt to
help his oppressed people, Israel, he found himself exiled to
the backwater country of Midian. There he found a wife and
spent the next four decades herding his father-in-law's sheep
(see Exodus 2:1–3:1; Acts 7:20–30).

All Moses' dreams had died. Ostracized from both his
kinsmen (Israel) and his adoptive country (Egypt), he
expected to live in obscurity until his dying day. And though
this was a giant step down from the grandeur for which he had
once seemed destined, it became comfortable and familiar.

Meanwhile, behind the scenes, God was using those
desert years to prepare the man for a role that was far more
important even than being king of Egypt.

ACT TWO, SCENE ONE

Moses awoke on this particular day, expecting to fill it much
as he had every other day during the past forty years—rise
with the sun and find grass for the sheep. As he roamed the
wilderness that day, Moses noticed that lightning had
apparently started a brushfire some ways off. Concerned for
the safety of his flock, he kept an eye on the smoke and flames,
until he noticed that only a single bush was burning. And it
wasn't burning up.

Little did he know, as he went to investigate, that God was about to launch him into the work for which he had been marked since birth.

Speaking from the burning bush, God presented the broken man with his next assignment—his new territory: "Come, and I will send you to Pharaoh that you may bring My people, the children of Israel, out of Egypt."

With that, Moses began to bob and weave. "Who am I that I should confront one of the world's most powerful men?"

For every excuse Moses could muster, God had an answer. *It has nothing to do with who you are, but who I am. I will be with you.*

And on it went, back and forth. God remained patient with Moses, accommodating his every doubt, until finally Moses played his last card: "Send someone else. Anyone. Just don't send me."

At that, the Bible says, "The anger of the LORD was kindled against Moses." God trumped Moses' final excuse, appointing Moses' brother Aaron as a spokesman to accompany him, and Moses gave in (see Exodus 3:10–4:17).

After forty years in familiar territory, Moses fought tooth-and-nail to avoid leaving his comfort zone. And God was angry at his reluctance. After all, God was promising to send His power and presence with Moses to complete the task!

You must make the decision to take a risk, to make a leap of faith.

And yet it was up to Moses to make the decision to break through. To take the risk. To make a leap of faith.

God gives you the same option. He will provide all the supernatural resources necessary to enlarge your territory, but *you* are the one who must decide to break out of your comfort zone. God builds the bridge across the chasm of impossibility, but it's up to you to accept the adventure and cross the bridge.

God won't change your heart against your will. He may give you every opportunity and every reason to change it. He might even use open confrontation, as He did with Moses and, centuries later, with Paul (see Acts 9). But the decision to act remains a matter of your will.

So as you think about the unknown territory God wants you to take, there's no need to wonder how you'll feel when the opportunity comes. You'll probably be scared.

Moses was.

I was. Over and over.

But God says, *Take courage. I'll be with you. Let's go!* He enables you to obey in spite of your fear.

GETTING PAST YOUR BORDER BULLIES

I don't want to mislead you. Once you decide to break out of your comfort zone, the hard part is not over. There at the edge of God's new territory, you will often encounter what I call your "border bullies." These are people who will push you back toward your comfort zone, trying to lead you back to "safety."

"You've never done that before," they cry.

"You don't know how."

"What about the money?"

"What will people say?"

"You're bound to fail."

"Just *try* crossing that line. You'll be sorry."

As if your own doubts weren't disheartening enough, along come these messages of discouragement from your enemies, your critics, and even well-intentioned friends and family!

When you're following God's will, He has promised to accompany you and to empower you to do what is right. But *you* must stand up to your border bullies. At first you may try reasoning with them, and you might even persuade some of them. In some cases, they may actually provide helpful input. But often you will simply have to push right past them.

When David faced Goliath, his brothers scoffed and King Saul voiced his doubts. But David looked back on God's past faithfulness in his life. In God's strength, David had defended his flock against lions and bears. So he stepped out boldly to confront this latest giant, saying, "The LORD, who delivered me from the paw of the lion and from the paw of the bear, He will deliver me from the hand of this Philistine" (1 Samuel 17:37).

In contrast, just one year after the Israelites' miraculous exodus out of Egypt, Moses sent twelve spies into the Promised Land—a land guaranteed them by God Almighty— and ten of the men came back to say it couldn't be done. They filed this report: "The land through which we have gone as spies is a land that devours its inhabitants, and all the people whom we saw in it are men of great stature... We were like grasshoppers in our own sight, and so we were in their sight" (Numbers 13:32–33).

From a human standpoint, these men were right. But from God's standpoint, they were faithless. As they cowered in fear, their own mental posture made them feel like insects before giants.

Yes, the wicked people inhabiting the land were an obstacle. But God said, *Do not fear! I will be with you.* Yet the ten unbelieving spies were border bullies for the rest of Israel, who gave in to them. The people had created in their own minds a big enemy and a small god whom they did not trust.

That generation died in the wilderness.

Their only lasting accomplishment was to raise children whose faithfulness would surpass their own.

GOD-EMPOWERED SWEAT

Fast-forward forty years. Of all the men in that faithless first generation, only two survived. When the other ten spies had voiced their disbelief, Joshua and Caleb were the two dissenting voices of faith. Thus Joshua became Moses' successor to lead Israel, at long last, into the Promised Land.

Now, even though Israel had decided to leave their comfort zone, and even though they had chosen to face down their border bullies, that didn't make the going easy. Three days before Israel's D-day, Joshua commanded the people, "Prepare provisions for yourselves, for within three days you will cross over this Jordan, to go in to possess the land which the LORD your God is giving you to possess" (Joshua 1:11).

So which is it? they may have thought. *Did God give us the land? Or do we have to fight to possess it?*

God had promised, "I will fight for you." Then He commanded Israel to go fight (see Deuteronomy 1:30, 41). Who did the fighting—God or Israel? The answer is *both*.

Taking new territory involves all of God *and* all of you. And if you leave out either part of this equation, your efforts will be ineffectual. Those who think it's all up to God will not accomplish anything. And those who think it's all up to us may never see the hand of God in action.

The work God gives you will often be *work*. He will

enlarge your territory, but you must struggle to occupy it. This runs contrary to the common misconception that when God is in something, it shouldn't be hard. In reality, when you venture out for God, toil and failure and misunderstanding most likely await you somewhere down the path. You may lie awake in bed, wondering whether you should ever have said yes to God. Some days you'll experience joy you never believed possible, while on others you'll feel desperately alone.

But you are never alone. And God is never limited. The heart of Jabez abhors the emptiness of a "safe" life. It asks for new territory, knowing how hard the going may be, but is willing to go there anyway—with God.

How Does He Do It?

Hopefully, by now you believe it's good to ask God for more territory. But what do His answers look like? What does God do in you in response, and how will you know when your territory is growing?

I see five primary ways in which He works in most instances. As we examine these, I'd like you to think about your life, your talents, your resources, and your opportunities. How might God work through you to do more for Him?

First, God enlarges your territory by increasing its size, enabling you to do something different or new. As Jesus was about to ascend into heaven, He left His followers with this assignment: "You shall receive power when the Holy Spirit has come upon you; and you shall be witnesses to Me in Jerusalem, and in all Judea and Samaria, and to the end of the earth" (Acts 1:8). Watch the geographical progression. They were first to proclaim the truth in Jerusalem, the heart of Judaism. Then they were to broaden out and do the same in all Judea, the surrounding region. Then further, into neighboring Samaria. And, ultimately, throughout every part of the globe.

More of the same in ever-widening circles.

Suppose you're a volunteer tutoring neighborhood kids in English as a second language (ESL). If you have ten regulars, why not brainstorm with God,

The heart of Jabez abhors the emptiness of a "safe" life.

plan a party, and ask Him to send you *twenty* kids? If God sends more, you may have to spend a little additional time or effort. But you can make a lifelong impact in several more lives.

God knows your capacity, and He will either expand your territory in such a way that your capacity remains sufficient or He'll increase your ability.

Second, God enlarges your territory by extending its scope, enabling you to do something new. One day, as Jesus walked by the Sea of Galilee, He saw brothers Simon Peter and Andrew fishing— and doing it well. They had grown up in the trade, after all. With that in mind, Jesus called to them, "Follow Me, and I will make you fishers of men" (Matthew 4:19). And that's what they became. In fact, in one day, Peter would help three thousand people enter into a new relationship with God (see Acts 2:41). Talk about a change of pace!

God doesn't often cause such a total about-face in a person's life. When He does, it can be extremely challenging. But if God is in it, He will hold your hand through it all. He may even show you undeveloped talents and gifts that were inside you all along.

More commonly, the new direction will be somehow related to what you're already doing. Let's go back to your ESL students. Suppose you pray for more territory. What God might do is send you another person who says, "I have no idea how to teach ESL; but if you will train me, I'd be happy to take half of your group." In addition to tutoring, now you're training tutors—and making an even greater impact for God.

NEW SKILLS, NEW APPROACH

Third, God enlarges your territory by sharpening your skills, enabling you to do what you do, better. Take a class. Read a book. Seek out a mentor who can share secrets from his or her experience. That's how an Irish-American musician named Michael discovered an opportunity to touch a life for God.

Although Michael played several instruments, he had only recently taken up bagpipes. He was playing his pipes at a club one night when a man named Jim asked if Michael knew a particular Irish tune. It happened to be one Michael had just learned, so he began to play. Upon hearing the mournful strains, Jim began to weep, and he moved to a corner table for privacy.

Michael finished the song, then went to sit with Jim. He learned that just one month earlier Jim had lost two cherished people in the same day—his father, to old age, and his best friend, in a terrible accident. The song Jim had requested was one of his father's favorites.

Michael recognized that God had opened a door by means of Michael's newly acquired musical skill, and he stepped through it, sharing God's comfort and love with the grieving man.[2]

What can you learn to do even more skillfully for God?

Fourth, God enlarges your territory by improving your strategy, enabling you to do something more effectively. We find one of the best examples of this in Exodus 18:13–27. Shortly after the people of Israel had been delivered from Egypt, Moses' father-in-law, Jethro, paid him a visit in the desert in order to see for himself the great nation Moses was leading and to hear the stories of God's mighty deeds. The day after he arrived, Jethro became increasingly dismayed as he watched Moses sit from morning until evening, mediating one dispute after another among the people.

That evening, Jethro pulled Moses aside and said, "What do you think you're doing? Both you and these people are going to wear yourselves out if you keep doing this alone."

He counseled Moses to select wise and trustworthy men, to whom he could delegate the majority of the lesser cases, hearing only the most important disputes himself. Moses saw the wisdom in the new strategy and implemented the changes immediately. In this way he was able to address the people's needs even more effectively, and he was also free to spend more time praying for the people and teaching them God's Word.

If your method is not working, or not working as well as it should, change it! Don't maintain the same routine just because that's the way you've always done it. Pray for wisdom. Invite suggestions from others. Brainstorm ideas. Try something new. If it doesn't work, you can go back to your original strategy or try something else. You may find that you can accomplish greater results with less effort.

STRATEGIC INVESTMENTS

Fifth and finally, God enlarges your territory by deepening its significance, enabling you to do something more influential. I once asked a man what he did to serve God. He told me he was gifted at helping people in practical ways, behind the scenes. But he also explained how God had begun to expand his territory.

At first he had been happy to lend aid to anyone. Then he was inspired to ask God to start sending him people to serve who were also placed in strategic leadership roles—godly people with unusual influence with large numbers of people. He wanted to support these influential people in order to enhance their effectiveness.

And God brought them. The man is still living his dream, doing what he has always enjoyed doing, but he is now investing his life with even greater eternal impact.

No one person is more important than any other. But God has endowed some individuals with greater influence (see Genesis 41:39–40). And some opportunities are better investments than others. I encourage you to ask God, "Please show me how to use my life for the greatest strategic impact." Then watch what He does.

I promise, you'll never be bored again.

PUBLISHER'S NOTE: You can learn more about stepping out of your comfort zone, confronting your border bullies, and living God's dream for your life in *The Dream Giver* by Bruce Wilkinson with David and Heather Kopp (Multnomah Publishers, 2004).

CHAPTER SEVEN

THE PRAYER FOR TERRITORY: LIVING IT OUT

I'm not asking you to be foolish; just outrageously, joyously confident in your God. He wants you to know the truth about His plans for you today: "My plans for you are only good. What I want for you is greater than anything you've seen so far. And you can trust Me completely!"[1]

THE PRAYER OF JABEZ DEVOTIONAL

Sitting and staring at the cell wall, Ryan knew that God was all he had left. An arson conviction could keep him locked up for several years. And the excuse that he had burned down the office building unintentionally, while drunk, was not likely to elicit any sympathy from the judge.

In that moment, Ryan's will broke, and he handed his life over to God.

His sentence turned out to be more lenient than expected—six months in treatment for alcohol addiction, then twelve months of jail time.

As the months passed, Ryan began to gain hope that he could do something important for God. During his first few weeks in jail, he spent much of his time studying his Bible. After a month he started a prayer meeting and then a Bible study for his cellblock.

One day Ryan began praying that God would expand his territory. That same day he alone, from among the 160 men on his cellblock, was invited to join a local pastor and some prison officers for a special Bible study. For three hours the pastor taught Ryan and the others the skills they needed to mine truth from God's Word. Ryan's view of Scripture was transformed.

With renewed enthusiasm, he returned to his cell and began to use his new training to teach scriptural truth to his fellow inmates while showing them how to study the Bible for themselves. His ministry thrived as he led many other men into new and deeper relationships with God.[2]

ORDINARY PEOPLE, EXTRAORDINARY LIVES

No matter what your situation, no matter how dark your history, God wants to use you to help fulfill His great plan. Call out to Him and He will powerfully expand your territory, wherever you are. And *who*ever you are.

The dream God gives you may seem way too big for you. But if it's truly from God, then it is doable! Although you and I have likely never met, I can say this with confidence because

Jesus promised, "I am with you always, even to the end of the age" (Matthew 28:20). Wherever you go, His powerful, steadfast presence goes with you.

Over the years I've been blessed with several wonderful friends whose grasp of God's Big Dream for their lives has been light years ahead of mine. I used to assume that these men and women belonged in a special category, set apart from the rest of us "normal" people. But as I grew to know them, I learned that they were just like you and me.

The difference? These "special" people routinely begged God to let them do more for Him.

Theirs was not just a fleeting request, but a persistent passion—a passion they asked God to plant in their hearts. How do you think God feels when His children come to Him and ask, "Please, do whatever You must in order that I might serve You more"? It fills His heart with joy!

It's time, then, to get down to the practical how-to's of praying for territory. In the next few pages, we'll look at six guidelines for doing it most effectively.

PRAYER AND PREPAREDNESS

First—and this may seem obvious—*pray earnestly for more territory.* Make it a daily habit. You've read about it, but don't stop there. Start praying!

Second, tell your family and friends about your commitment. When God starts answering your prayers, your life will never be the same. So help those around you understand the changes they're seeing in your life. And since we're not designed to grow in isolation, you'll also need someone to encourage you at those times when you're tempted to lose sight of God's dream.

Third, learn to recognize a "Jabez moment." Keep your antenna constantly alert for divine appointments, through which you can touch a life or do something for God's purposes. Keep asking God, "What's next?"

Burton, a police investigator with the State of California, had been praying for just such an opportunity. That's why he was ready when it came.

Be prepared for "Jabez moments," through which you may touch the life of another.

His new chief had organized a three-day conference to build rapport within the department. The opening session included several icebreakers, one of which was a mock game show requiring contestants to guess the identities of coworkers based on little-known facts about their lives and backgrounds.

When the question "Which employee has a theology degree?" appeared on the overhead screen, Burton wondered, *Who could have known about that?* With a little guidance, the man in the hot seat correctly guessed Burton's name.

At that point, many Christians in Burton's shoes would have tried to disappear, embarrassed for being identified as "religious." But not Burton. He rose to the opportunity. Swarmed with questions during the break, he talked enthusiastically with curious coworkers. Throughout the weekend he was able to discuss God freely with many of the 150 people in attendance.

Burton is now considered the unofficial "chaplain" of his department, all because of one simple icebreaker. And because he was ready when God opened the door.[3]

FLEXIBLE FAITH

Fourth, accept service opportunities that stretch your faith. Don't run away. Watch for territory you can take only by trusting God. Feeling inadequate? That's because you are. God is your adequacy (see 2 Corinthians 3:5). You will grow in faith when you let Him show Himself powerful in you.

While we're on this point, may I speak directly to a special category of people—to those who think their usefulness has ended? I'm referring to those of you who are in a later season of life.

Friends, there's still more ground to take. Why fritter away these years when you could not just walk or run, but *accelerate* across the finish line?

Earlier I mentioned two faithful men who survived Israel's faithless first generation and were privileged to enter the Promised Land. Joshua was one. Caleb was the other.

Several years into the conquest, when Israel controlled most of their new land, Caleb stood with Joshua and pointed to a mountain stronghold, still occupied by the wicked people of Canaan. He said, "Here I am this day, eighty-five years old. Now therefore, give me this mountain of which the LORD spoke in that day; for you heard in that day how the Anakim were there, and that the cities were great and fortified. It may be that the LORD will be with me, and I shall be able to drive them out as the LORD said" (Joshua 14:10, 12).

Caleb was eighty-five! And he still wanted to grab more for God!

If you're past retirement, you may not realize that your adventure continues. Just think of the resources you have at your disposal! Time, wisdom, experience.

And a mighty God.

GUIDE YOUR GIFTING AND GLORIFY GOD

The *fifth* practical guideline for praying for territory is this: *Reprioritize your time, talents, and treasure.* Take the very same resources you are using for other purposes and use them as effectively as possible for God.

Once I was talking with a vice president of marketing for a large Atlanta corporation, and I asked him, "Do you ever use your marketing skills for ministry?"

He wasn't sure what I meant, so I asked him about his church. He told me that three hundred people attended there. I asked, "Can you use your marketing skills to double your church's attendance in three months?"

"Sure," he replied without hesitation, "that's simple. I could design a marketing plan to draw three hundred people to church easily. Where I work, that would be a simple task. But I never imagined using my business talents here at the church."

What about the gifts, resources, and opportunities God has placed in your hands? How might you use them for the purposes nearest God's heart?

Sixth and finally, build up God's reputation by crediting Him openly. When God does something great in your life, take the focus off yourself and shine the spotlight on Him. Telling what He has done will help other people find joy and motivation to trust Him more.

CATCH HOLD OF GOD'S DREAM

I remember a very unique Promise Keepers event at which I was privileged to speak. The setting was a big, open stadium in Fresno, California, with seating for forty-five thousand. I arrived in advance and walked into the stadium. Immediately, I felt overwhelmed with a sense of God's power and presence, and I said aloud to myself, "God's going to do something truly miraculous today."

But I wasn't sure why. Then I saw a group of people sitting and praying together in the stands. I went and sat behind them until they were finished, and I said to the nearest man, "Sir, I sense the presence of the Lord here. Do you?"

"Oh, yes," he said. "We all do!"

I asked, "Do you know why it is so strong?"

"Well," he said, "when we learned that Promise Keepers was coming to Fresno, people from seventy-five different churches began meeting every Friday night for an hour and a half for a whole year. We prayed that God would move strongly in our area and that masses of men would experience revolutionary life change."

That night the response was such that no amount of human effort could explain it. When challenged to renew their commitment to God, thousands upon thousands of men completely filled the stadium floor, and they kept coming until they filled every aisle all the way to the very top of the stadium. God worked greatly because His people prayed, *Lord, enlarge our territory.*

Now come with me and catch a glimpse of another, even bigger gathering. In eternity. The earthly stadium in Fresno, filled with tens of thousands, will be a mere droplet in the sea of people we see in heaven:

> After these things I looked, and behold, a great multitude which no one could number, of all nations, tribes, peoples, and tongues, standing before the throne and before the Lamb, clothed with white robes, with palm branches in their hands, and crying

out with a loud voice, saying, "Salvation belongs to our God who sits on the throne, and to the Lamb!"

REVELATION 7:9–10

God has shown us how our story ends—with countless people from every nation on earth crying out joyfully to God. What part of that throng will be there because of you? What part of God's dream is linked to your destiny?

Just think what a difference you could make in many, many lives if you were to pray passionately and faithfully for enlarged territory from God, for God. Imagine the miraculous divine partnership that will grow out of your plea, *Let me accomplish more for You.* With His infinite ability and your willing availability, He can literally do anything (see 1 Corinthians 6:19–20; Ephesians 2:8–10).

We look back on events in the Bible and on certain periods of history, and we see great exploits for God performed at the hands of people we call "the giants of the faith." But the only real Giant in the picture is God, and He hasn't changed. He used absolutely ordinary people then, and He will do the same today in your generation.

And after you and your Master are finished with all He has entrusted to your hands, you will stand before Him in heaven's throne room. On that day, because you asked boldly for greater ministry impact, and because you stepped forward courageously in spite of your fear, you'll experience an eternity of joy enhanced by the knowledge that people are there because you prayed. You'll bask in a reward that we can't even begin to comprehend.

And the Lord will smile on you and say, "Well done."

POWER FROM GOD

And Jabez called on the God of Israel saying,
"Oh, that You would bless me indeed,
and enlarge my territory,
that Your hand would be with me,
and that You would keep me from evil,
that I may not cause pain!"
So God granted him what he requested.

People Who Prayed

AN OFFER WE COULDN'T REFUSE

by Jim and Carol Smith

Our friend Larry George is a retired banker—a man of great compassion and even greater faith. In 1993 he followed the Lord's direction and bought a twenty-by-thirty-foot building in Port Moresby, Papua New Guinea. There he founded the Port Moresby Mission, offering emergency shelter for local street kids.

When we left our home in Australia to work with Larry, we found as many as 120 youths housed in the tiny building. Those young men received temporary food and shelter from the mission, but compared to the real need, we knew that we were applying a Band-Aid to a severed artery.

The mission staff prayed for wisdom. The Lord gave Larry a vision for a vocational and agricultural school, and we were able to purchase some farmland outside of Port Moresby. Not only did we provide food and shelter at the farm, but we also taught the boys skills—such as reading, writing, agriculture, and animal husbandry—that could keep them off the streets.

In the spring of 2001, we came across *The Prayer of Jabez*. We were struck with the prayer's simplicity and began asking the Lord for a desperately needed expansion in Port Moresby. Within days, an anonymous benefactor supplied the school with the funds to tear down an existing building and rebuild one that met our needs.

The Lord also put it on our hearts to start a shelter for young women. We also prayed about opening a clinic for abused children.

Our benefactor learned of our need and told us to start searching for a suitable piece of property. The only thing we could find was a building in the most exclusive part of the city, appraised at $1 million—twice the amount our benefactor had offered us.

The staff gathered to pray.

"I think we are supposed to offer $491,000," Larry informed us matter-of-factly.

"Where did you come up with that figure?" a puzzled staff member asked.

"From the chapter and verse references for the prayer of Jabez: 1 Chronicles 4:9–10," Larry replied. "I feel that is the amount the Lord would have us offer."

So Larry made the offer, and we all kept praying.

By God's miraculous intervention, we won the bid! Our benefactor supplied the money, and the mission once again expanded its borders.

We then hired a master carpenter, who is training our boys in carpentry. They are making all the furniture for the new Women's and Children's Centers.

The boys are so excited about the new skills they are learning. More of them are leaving the mission and getting jobs, rather than returning to life on the streets! We are filling their stomachs and minds, and they are leaving this place with a passion for God.

Although Papua New Guinea is undergoing great political turmoil, we at the Port Moresby Mission continue to experience the Lord's hand upon our work. We are still praying the prayer of Jabez, and we are being blessed beyond measure.

CHAPTER EIGHT

THE HAND OF GOD: A CLOSER LOOK

The Dreamers I know who are changing the world know
a secret: God is eager to show Himself strong toward
Dreamers who take risks to do what He wants done.[1]

THE DREAM GIVER

*I*magine you're climbing a mountain that is far beyond your
skill level.

And you're stuck.

Clinging desperately to meager handholds and footholds,
you find yourself unable to move forward or backward. Your
arms and legs begin to tremble uncontrollably. You don't
know how much longer you can hold on.

Then your guide—an experienced mountaineer—
reaches out and grips your hand. Your courage is bolstered by
his reassuring voice. "It's okay. I've got you. Just grab hold over
here. Pull yourself slowly up. That's good."

Clinging desperately to his hand, you eventually reach a secure perch.

Drawing repeatedly upon his strength, you finally achieve the summit. You know that without your guide's helping hand, you would never have made it.

That's much the way we experience the hand of God in our lives. But take note: The hand of God comes consistently into play only for those who climb mountains.

After you have begun asking for enlarged territory, you will see your ministry opportunities expand and your dream begin to be realized. Your territory (your sphere of influence) will burst right past your comfort zone, bowling over your border bullies, and suddenly you'll find yourself facing a task that you know is humanly impossible.

That's when you're ready for part 3 of the prayer of Jabez: "Oh...that Your hand would be with me" (1 Chronicles 4:10). In essence, this is saying, *Lord, I can't do this. If You don't put Your hand upon me, it's all going to fall apart.*

Have you ever felt this way? Has God ever taken you to the point where you know your best efforts are doomed to failure unless He comes through? Unfortunately, many people have never come to this, because they've never ventured beyond where they feel safe. These people will seldom, if ever, see God working powerfully in their lives.

The hand of God is released when we dare to step outside our comfort zones to serve Him. That's why His hand of power comes through for those who've learned to pray, *Lord, let me do more for You—a lot more! Show me Your big dream for me.*

When you launch into this adventure of faith, you discover the exhilaration of loving and serving God. Now you're not just reading about the miraculous life or watching it fulfilled in someone else. You're *living* it!

JABEZ'S THIRD REQUEST

What did Jabez mean when he asked, "Oh...that Your hand would be with me"? Let's look closer at the two components of his request.

First, the "hand" of God implies *God's power*. When God's hand is mentioned in the Bible, we see Him doing something powerful. For example, it was God's hand that parted the Red Sea and later the Jordan River for the children of Israel to cross (see Joshua 4:23–24). When the Philistines stole the ark of God's covenant, the hand of God brought judgment upon them in the form of terrible disease and destruction (see 1 Samuel 5:9–11).

In Old Testament Hebrew, there are two different words for *hand*. One refers to a *closed* hand, and the other to an *open* hand—the latter implying that God's power is not withheld but unleashed, usually immediately. In his prayer, Jabez used the word for an open hand. He was asking the Lord, *Please release Your mighty power here and now.*

As the second component of his request, Jabez asked that God's hand "would be with me." In other words, Jabez was asking God to act on his behalf—not just in any direction or for any purpose, but toward Jabez himself and for the purpose of enabling Jabez to manage his new territory.

With that understanding in mind, let's look close at five distinctives of what it means to have the hand of God be with us.

MIRACLES WITH HEART

First, the hand of God is not merely God's power, but God's person. When you pray for power, remember that you're not talking to a machine or some impersonal force. He is your Father. And when God acts on your behalf, He doesn't do it from afar; He is personally present, closely involved with you and interested in your concerns.

Second, the hand of God is not mere human ingenuity, but divine intervention. The hand of God breaks through into our world—into our time and space—and performs His will in such a way that we can only shake our heads in amazement and say, "Look at what God did!"

Third, the hand of God is not natural, but supernatural, doing that which only God can do: the miraculous.

Let me clarify what I mean by the word *miracle*. Some people believe miracles occur only when God breaks the laws of nature. But in Scripture, God performed many of His miracles by powerfully guiding the forces of nature, not by superseding them. For example, when Jesus commanded the storm to be calm (see Matthew 8:23–27), He supernaturally advanced the schedule for what would have happened eventually anyway. No laws were broken, yet it was an act that only God could have done. A miracle.

Some miracles *do* break the laws of nature. But more often God works in harmony with nature. We recognize these actions as miracles because they "just happen" to come in response to our prayers, in God's perfect timing.

MIRACLES WITH PURPOSE

Fourth, the hand of God is not guided by my wishes, but by His will. God always does what He chooses to do. Because He is good, our

> *Dare to ask, "Lord, please release Your mighty power here and now."*

wishes and His will often coincide, so that He frequently does what we request.

On the other hand, sometimes we learn that our desires—even pure desires—run contrary to God's will. He doesn't mind our expressing those wishes; He always wants to hear the honest expressions of our hearts. But He will always do what He wants to do, because His will is wisest and best. And He is always good.

MIRACLES WITH IMPACT

The fifth and final distinctive: *The hand of God is not evidenced by feelings, but by actions.* Some people who pray for God's power don't believe He has exercised it unless they *feel* something. They expect to feel some special emotion or physical sensation, and when it doesn't come, they lose faith that God has done anything.

Sometimes when God moves, His presence is almost palpable. Other times He will move in power, and you won't notice anything unusual until after the fact.

The one guaranteed constant with the hand of God is *action.* The movement of His hand always results in miraculous change. Whether God's activity occurs within your person or in your circumstances, His hand brings change in the way things *are,* not necessarily in the way you feel.

MODERN MIRACLES

Earlier we dealt with some of the misconceptions that have arisen about praying for blessing since the original release of

The Prayer of Jabez. Now I want to look at three misconceptions about praying for power. As we examine these, notice how subtle but significant the difference between error and truth can be.

HAND OF GOD MISCONCEPTION #1:
*Only in the Bible do people experience
the hand of God.*

I remember, years ago, reading Bible stories and spiritual biographies of great men and women of God, and yearning to experience the hand of God! Again and again, I would pray, *Lord, why won't You let me see Your great power unleashed? Why can't I live it rather than only reading about it?*

I'm happy to say that my doubts didn't keep God from answering.

A few months ago I met with a group of hundreds of university students from twelve nations. It happened on Tuesday night of the last week of an intense monthlong initiative in Swaziland, where these young people had spent a full week visiting every single high school in the nation to teach abstinence as the primary method for HIV prevention. You should have heard the students as they glowingly shared remarkable and even miraculous stories of what God had done during that week.

When it was my turn to speak, I shared a major concern facing our faith-based humanitarian organization, Dream for Africa. We had set our sights on recruiting ten thousand American volunteers to come to Africa during the next year, but we were told by the airlines that travel arrangements on this scale would be problematic. And so I asked the students to join with us and pray that God would provide Dream for Africa with a 747 jet.

Laughter erupted across the room as the students shook their heads in disbelief.

"Let me ask you a question," I said to the audience, as the laughter died down. "Let's say you had run out of money and needed funds to buy food to eat. So you prayed and asked God to supply as He promised. Or let's say that you had run out of seats and needed a 747 to carry thousands of volunteers to Africa. So you prayed and asked God to supply as He promised.

"Which would be more difficult for God to provide," I asked, "the food or the 747? Would He say, 'The food is no problem, and maybe I can find you a small four-seater. But a 747, you've got to be joking'?"

The silence in the room shouted that the students had seen the root of their unbelief. One thing was not harder than another for God. God doesn't know the word *hard*!

Two nights later, at midnight, my phone rang. It was a friend from the States. He said a corporation that wished to remain anonymous had decided to purchase a 747 jet for Dream for Africa.

The truth is, the hand of God is still available to us. Yet many people in the Bible thought that the power of God was no longer available in *their* day. Gideon, for example, lived during a dark and confusing time in Israel's history—a period during which God's chosen people had strayed from their faith. Indeed, God's powerful hand was mightily at work in their midst—He was actively chastising the nation by allowing the Midianites to oppress them. God was seeking to wake His people from their disobedience and bring them back to Himself.

One day, the angel of the Lord appeared to Gideon and said, "The LORD is with you, you mighty man of valor!" (Judges 6:12).

Gideon must have had to stifle a cynical laugh at this. He answered, "If the LORD is with us, why then has all this happened to us? And where are all His miracles which our fathers told us about?" (verse 13).

And so God persuaded this disillusioned young man, through a series of miracles, that He was still present and powerful in the midst of His people. Gideon led a revival in Israel, and with renewed faith, the people began calling on God. As a result, they were privileged once again to see His mighty hand intervening in history as He miraculously rescued them from their oppressive enemy.

Ask for His hand to be with you and step out in faith.

Like Gideon, many today are saying, "Why don't we see miracles? All we have are stories from the past." These are people who have never experienced the powerful hand of God in their lives. Perhaps they have never ventured out beyond their comfort zones for God. Being addicted to their own security, they feel no need to ask for the hand of God.

Take the risk and give God a chance. Ask for His hand to be with you and step out in faith. He will show up. Even today.

STAY IN THE WAY

When I explain this next misconception, you may wonder if we're reading the same Bible. But stay with me.

HAND OF GOD MISCONCEPTION #2:
You must surrender complete control to experience the hand of God.

Yes, you read it correctly. This is a misconception, a half-truth. Let me explain what I mean.

One school of thought, to which many genuinely committed Christians subscribe, is rooted in a fervent desire to be used by God (that's good) and the recognition that we can't accomplish anything of significance apart from God (that's true). *I am limited and sinful*, the reasoning goes. *I'd better get out of the way so God won't be hindered as He works in my life.*

And so these sincere followers of Christ conclude that if they surrender their minds and bodies to the full control of the Holy Spirit, He will exercise more of His power though them. Sounds good, but errors can innocently slip into our thinking and behavior at this point.

The Bible clearly teaches that we are to submit wholly to the will of God, but nowhere does it say that we are to abandon discernment and self-control. Discernment has been given to us for the very purpose of determining which messages and actions are from Him and which are not. As for self-control, Galatians 5:23 tells us it is one of the fruits of the Holy Spirit's work in our lives. In other words, self-control is evidence of the presence of the Spirit! Never seek the power of God by abandoning your self-control, physically or mentally, because His hand is demonstrated through the work of the Spirit, which is demonstrated by your *self*-control.

As far as your mind is concerned, Paul explains that our responsibility is to bring "every thought into captivity to the obedience of Christ" (2 Corinthians 10:5). That doesn't mean emptying your thoughts or surrendering control over what you think to God. Instead, you are to exercise self-control over every thought you permit your mind to think.

The truth is, *in order for the hand of God to work through you, you must exercise control over your body and your mind with the strength He provides.* You are an intelligent instrument in God's hand. He has purposefully endowed you with a personality, a mind, and a will in order that He might use them for His work.

Keep thinking. Keep discerning. Keep making decisions as wisely as possible, in prayerful dependence on God, and He will use you *by means of* your thoughts and your self-controlled actions.

HE'S THE SOURCE

Let's say you've experienced the hand of God working powerfully in your life over a period of time. You can hardly believe the miracles! This is a situation where you become especially vulnerable to a third misconception regarding the hand of God.

At some point you may be awed by the contrast between the accomplishments you're seeing now and how little happened in the earlier days of your faith. The error creeps in when you begin to think, *I'm more powerful than I used to be.* At that point you've succumbed to the third misconception.

> HAND OF GOD MISCONCEPTION #3:
> *You gain spiritual power the more God uses you.*

Simon Peter had to confront this same error one day in Jerusalem when he and John met a lame man begging at the temple gate. In response to their faith, the hand of God worked through them to heal the man's legs. Word of the miracle spread quickly, and people came running from every direction.

The crowd was amazed. Astonished. Filled with wonder.

But they missed the point. The onlookers thought it was Peter and John who had done this great thing.

Quickly perceiving the problem, Peter spoke to the crowd. "Men of Israel, why do you marvel at this? Or why look so intently at us"— *now catch this* —"as though by our *own power* or *godliness* we had made this man walk? [Christ's] name, through faith in His name, has made this man strong" (Acts 3:12, 16).

Peter was saying, first, that he himself possessed absolutely no power to heal. None! Peter the apostle of Christ had no more supernatural ability than Peter the career fisherman.

The same is true for you. Certainly some amazing changes occur when you begin your new life with Christ. You are given a new heart for God, and the Holy Spirit comes to live within you. Incredible! But you are still only human, not superhuman. When miracles happen in your life, the difference is not who you are, but who is with you and in you (see Acts 15:12).

And don't miss the second element Peter mentioned. Some people think the more godly they become the more power they will have. Peter knew that the degree of his godliness didn't cause him to have any more or less power. Whether godly or ungodly, your power remains the same. The hand of God can and does work through the godly, the carnal, and the ungodly. Just a surface reading of the Scriptures demonstrates that.

The truth is, *the hand of God, not your godliness, produces power in your life.*

What does godliness do for us? It makes us more like Christ in character. And it draws us nearer to the God of miracles.

God can certainly do anything He wants, using anyone

He wants, whether they are godly or not. But as we will see in the next chapter, what God enjoys most is laying His hand on His children—especially those who long to become godly instruments of His power.

CHAPTER NINE

THE HAND OF GOD: GOING DEEPER

God has chosen the foolish things of the world to put
to shame the wise, and God has chosen the weak things
of the world to put to shame the things which are mighty; that,
as it is written, "He who glories, let him glory in the LORD."

1 CORINTHIANS 1:27, 31

*M*ental whiplash.

What better way to describe the experience of Jesus' followers as they watched the amazing reversal unfolding before their eyes? An hour ago they had been mourning the death of the Messiah. With Him had died the dream He promised to fulfill.

Now, suddenly, He was standing among them in the flesh!

"Touch Me," He invited them. "I am real. Give Me something to eat."

The group was shocked and afraid, unwilling to believe their senses. But joy slowly seeped through as Jesus began to teach them.

He turned the disciples' attention toward the future and described the mission they must spend the rest of their lifetimes beginning to fulfill: "that repentance and remission of sins should be preached in His name to all nations, beginning at Jerusalem" (Luke 24:47).

Now fear returned like a sudden winter freeze. This mismatched band of outcasts? Teach God's truth to the whole world? They exchanged nervous glances, torn between wanting to believe and wanting to escape.

The Master understood. "Don't worry," He said. "I don't want you to start quite yet, because you're not ready. Wait a little while."

The tension eased a bit.

Then Jesus continued, "Behold, I send the Promise of My Father upon you; but tarry in the city of Jerusalem until you are endued with power from on high" (v. 49).

The Promise? Power from on high?

Only a short time later they would understand what Jesus meant. On that day, this little group of downtrodden misfits would begin to do the impossible, bringing thousands at a time to new faith in God. Because the hand of God, in the personal presence of His Holy Spirit, would be with them.

But for now, in the upper room where they gathered, Jesus' followers were powerless to fulfill His vision until He provided the means. Fulfilling God's big dream was God's task; only God could make it happen.

And so the fledgling church learned that the hand of God is required for the work of God (see also Acts 1:8; 11:21).

He Wants to Work Where?

"That's wonderful!" some might say. "I'll start praying for the hand of God, and then I'll sit back and watch Him do His thing. This should be interesting."

But there's a problem with that approach. Life with God is not a spectator sport. If you pray for the hand of God, you should expect to see His power working *through you and your active service.*

In Colossians 1:29, the apostle Paul, who was well known for his impact on thousands of lives throughout the known world, explained how he was able to accomplish so much: "To this end I also labor, striving according to His working which works in me mightily." See the blend of human responsibility and divine power? *I labor and strive while God works in me mightily.*

This principle applies to everyone who seeks to impact the world for God. You were designed to live your life constantly in His supernatural power. If you don't, you'll perform without real effect, as though the hand of God were not available to you. Your efforts will not advance God's reputation. You'll never experience the thrill of watching God part the clouds and come down to do a work that could only be His.

And you may never realize what you're missing.

Faith and the Hand of God

I once led a conference with fifty leaders who oversee thousands of Christian workers around the world. I grouped them around seven tables and asked them to brainstorm the three biggest reasons that we don't see God's power released.

After ten minutes, I asked the first table, "What's your number one reason?"

The answer: "Unbelief."

When I asked for clarification, they explained, "We may pray, but we don't really believe that God is going to intervene, that He wants to intervene, or that He even has the power."

Interesting. I moved on and asked the same question of table two.

They answered, "Unbelief."

The room became quiet. This was shocking because we hadn't been discussing unbelief.

Table three: "Unbelief."

Table four: "Unbelief."

And on it went. Table six listed unbelief as the second reason. Every other group had placed it at the top of their list.

Unbelief sets you up for defeat before you even start.

This gathering of leaders, all experienced in high-impact service for God, agreed that *the hand of God is hindered by the sin of unbelief.*

Unbelief sets you up for defeat before you even start. That's also what God's Word says. In Matthew 13:54–58, we find Jesus, after a period of successful ministry throughout the region of Galilee, returning to His hometown of Nazareth. You might think his accomplishments would earn Him a warm reception, but instead, the hometown folk took offense at Him. Matthew tells us, "He did not do many mighty works there because of their unbelief."

Later the disciples attempted unsuccessfully to cast a demon out of a boy, as Jesus had given them authority to do.

When they asked Him about their failure, He answered that it was because of their "unbelief" (Matthew 17:20).

Then Jesus continued, "I say to you, if you have faith as a mustard seed, you will say to this mountain, 'Move from here to there,' and it will move; *and nothing will be impossible for you*" (emphasis added).

Can you believe that? If you can, you will see God's hand working through your life, because God's power knows no limitations.

How can you know when you're truly believing? Don't wait for a feeling. Pray for guidance and power and then obey. That's how you will *show* that you believe.

PICK A NEED, ANY NEED

Okay, let's suppose you're praying and stepping out in faith and the hand of God begins to work in your life. What exactly can you expect to happen? In the Bible we find that God's hand intervenes in our lives in primarily five ways.

First, the hand of God intervenes to make provision. Have you ever found yourself in a predicament where you thought maybe God couldn't—or wouldn't—come through with something you needed? Money? People? Basic needs for survival?

This is one of our most common fears. *Maybe God isn't strong enough, or doesn't care enough, to provide for this size of a problem.*

Even Moses, a man of great faith, struggled with this fear. Israel had been in the desert for about a year and they were becoming noisily tired of the Manna Diet. However, the problem was not nutritional, but attitudinal. Moses feared an insurrection if God didn't provide a change of pace in the menu.

God told Moses to pass on a message: "Consecrate yourselves for tomorrow, and you shall eat meat," He said. "You shall eat, not one day, nor two days, nor five days, nor ten days, nor twenty days, but for a whole month" (Numbers 11:18–20).

At this, Moses responded with unbelief. He had seen God perform many incredible wonders—the ten plagues, the parting of the Red Sea, the daily provision of manna. But here was a promise even God couldn't keep! So Moses said to God:

> "The people whom I am among are six hundred thousand men on foot [perhaps two million men, women, and children total]; yet You have said, 'I will give them meat, that they may eat for a whole month.' Shall flocks and herds be slaughtered for them, to provide enough for them? Or shall all the fish of the sea be gathered together for them, to provide enough for them?"
>
> VV. 21–22

I love God's answer.

"Has the LORD's arm been shortened?" He demanded (verse 23). *Do you think My power has diminished? I'm the one who spoke the birds and fish into existence in a day. And you think I couldn't do it again? What? Do you think I've grown old and helpless?*

God kept His promise, of course.

Isn't it amazing that—no matter how many times we've seen God provide in the past—when we face the next bigger challenge we doubt His sufficiency?

I saw the hand of God at work providing for an old friend of mine at Amelia Island, Florida, late one night at a Christian conference. Earlier, I had tried to comfort and encourage him, but with no success. He was a patriarch, now in his early eighties and still serving God with all his heart. When the meeting ended, I tried to find him, but he had already left.

After the session a couple of men wanted to speak to me, so we sat down at a small table in the hotel hallway. It was getting late and we were wrapping up the conversation when I saw my old friend walking slowly down the corridor toward us, head down, shoulders stooped. I invited him to join us.

"What's bothering you, Doc?" I asked.

"Oh, nothing much, I guess."

I sensed that God had brought him back because He was going to do something special for this man. "I've know you for a long time," I said, "and it's clear that something is weighing heavily on your heart."

Slowly, he looked up and with a sigh of resignation began, "You know that youth conference center that I've been building on the side of that mountain? Well, we ran out of money about six months ago, and it looks like my dream isn't going to come true after all."

"Doc, you've started a number of major Christian organizations over your long and fruitful lifetime, and they are still having a great impact after all these years. The youth conference center would be no different than that; why wouldn't God want it finished? How much do you need?"

"Lots."

"More than $10,000? More than $50,000?"

"I need $150,000."

It was one of those rare moments when none of us could miss the presence of God. I reached for one of my business cards, turned it over, wrote something down, and put it into my shirt pocket. God was up to something. His hand was moving.

Within two minutes, another man came walking down the otherwise-deserted hallway. It was 10:30 at night and there was no reason for him to be there. I called out, "Bill, come and join us!" I had met Bill (not his real name) once before on a trip to Russia and knew him to be a generous businessman. "Do you know about the youth conference center Doc is building?" Bill nodded in affirmation. "Well, he needs some money, and I'm praying that God sent you over here to give it to him. He needs $150,000."

Bill tipped his chair back and folded his arms. "A hundred and fifty thousand—that's a lot of money. There's no way."

Slowly, I reached into my pocket, pulled out my business card, and handed it to Bill. I smiled and said, "The Lord knew you were going to need this. Turn it over and read what it says on the other side."

He read aloud, "10:25 P.M. Dear God, please send Bill back to give Doc $150,000."

The other two men with us yelled in celebration—that's how we all feel when the hand of God is unleashed.

"Well then, the Lord made that clear," Bill said. He smiled at Doc and said, "You'll have the $150,000 next week."

The Bible clearly states, "My God shall supply all your need according to His riches in glory by Christ Jesus" (Philippians 4:19).

You have no need that God cannot provide for.

WHO'S THE BOSS?

Second, the hand of God intervenes to move the hearts of those in power. Kings? Presidents? Dictators? Emperors? They're all under God's sovereign rulership. Proverbs 21:1 assures us, "The king's heart is in the hand of the LORD, like the rivers of water; He turns it wherever He wishes."

God did this for Nehemiah when, at the end of Israel's exile, Nehemiah went to the king of Persia—the most powerful man in the world, who had no vested interest in Israel's fortunes—and asked him to provide letters of permission and large amounts of money to rebuild the city of Jerusalem. Nehemiah prayed that God would move the king's heart, and indeed the king honored all of Nehemiah's requests (see Nehemiah 2:1–8).

This is the kind of thing God can do when all the other details and provisions have fallen into place, but the person in charge says no.

Back in the early 1990s, after the Soviet Union collapsed and the Iron Curtain opened up, a total of eighty-seven Christian groups joined forces in a massive effort to send Christian teachers to teach Christian morals and ethics across that vast land. Many doors had dramatically opened, but in the midst of a major pastor's conference in Phoenix, news came that a hostile group had convinced the Russian national leadership to ban our efforts. We were devastated.

One man said to me, "It's over—and we thought this would be a major movement for God!" Others were weeping openly. We had put so much of our lives into this, and now the opportunity was gone.

Our only recourse was to pray. We went to our knees and begged God to change the minds of those in power. For two hours we pleaded with God on behalf of the people of Russia.

Then word came, right there in that same meeting: "We're in! The leadership of the nation just overruled them and reinstated permission for us to come!"

Often you need not fight against those in authority. Just go over their heads to the Ruler of the universe.

Third, the hand of God intervenes with His presence. One of my favorite Bible stories is found in 2 Kings 6, where Elisha and his servant found themselves surrounded by a huge, hostile army. Elisha's servant panicked, but the prophet calmly said, "Do not fear, for those who are with us are more than those who are with them." Then Elisha looked up to the One who commands the angels and said, "LORD, I pray, open his eyes that he may see."

The Bible says, "Then the LORD opened the eyes of the young man, and he saw. And behold, the mountain was full of horses and chariots of fire all around Elisha" (2 Kings 6:15–17).

God came in a special *show* of His power, in order to remind the servant, *I'll never leave or forsake you.*

One of the greatest spiritual revivals in history happened in the Great Awakening in eighteenth-century New England. A number of miraculous events are reliably documented in the historical records. God manifested His presence so powerfully in some towns that people would simply enter the town and feel irresistibly compelled to climb out of their carriages, kneel in the road, and cry out for a changed life. One ship from England came within a mile and a half of shore, when suddenly all onboard fell to their knees and begged God for forgiveness.

When God shows up, everything changes.

SAFE IN HIS HAND

Fourth, the hand of God intervenes to defend and protect. On the night before His crucifixion, Jesus was brought before Pilate, but refused to respond to any of the Roman's questions. Finally the frustrated ruler said, "Do You not know that I have power to crucify You, and power to release You?"

Listen to Jesus' answer as He stood there, beaten and bloody: "You could have no power at all against Me unless it had been given you from above" (John 19:10–11).

Although He was going voluntarily to His death, Jesus knew that His Father had the power to protect Him.

A few years ago I was in the Philippines with my daughter, Jennifer, teaching at a leadership conference. When I had finished, we were offered as a thank-you gift an overnight stay at a beautiful resort in the cool mountains. I was exhausted, and both Jennifer and I eagerly anticipated the father-daughter time.

But at the last minute I was asked to forego our getaway and teach one more day. Jennifer and I prayed about it and, with heavy hearts, we came to the conclusion that God wanted us to stay. We were two very disappointed travelers at that moment.

The next day, as I was teaching leaders from fifty-four different nations on the sixth floor of a high-rise hotel in downtown Manila, a very powerful earthquake struck. The sixteen-story hotel shook violently, the plaster walls split and crashed, and the group across the hall was screaming in terror. I thought the building would surely collapse on us, as it seemed the quake would never end.

Finally, it subsided and we thanked God for His protection.

But I had no idea just how dramatically God had protected us until later that afternoon. The conference leader came to me and said, "Do you know where the epicenter of the earthquake took place? In the very resort town where you were supposed to be staying today. In fact, we just received word that everyone in the hotel wing where you were scheduled to stay has been tragically killed."

Pray for and trust God's protecting hand.

ADEQUACY FROM ABOVE

Fifth, the hand of God intervenes to overcome your personal limitations.
Anytime you face a big task—especially one that seems
impossible—you come face-to-face with the reality that you
are a limited being. But be careful not to project your
inadequacies onto God. Just because you can't, that doesn't
mean He can't.

Paul wrote about the lesson he learned when a malady
had left him fragile and weak:

> [God] said to me, "My grace is sufficient for you, for
> My strength is made perfect in weakness." Therefore
> most gladly I will rather boast in my infirmities, that
> the power of Christ may rest upon me. Therefore I
> take pleasure in infirmities, in reproaches, in needs, in
> persecutions, in distresses, for Christ's sake. For when
> I am weak, then I am strong.
>
> 2 CORINTHIANS 12:9–10

This is the same man who later wrote, "I can do all
things"—not because I'm adequate, but because Jesus is—
"through Christ who strengthens me" (Philippians 4:13).

God is not looking to us to display strength or ability;
those resources come from Him. What He's looking for is
loyalty.

For much of my life, I thought that I longed for God to
intervene more than He did. Somehow I thought that He was
preoccupied in heaven and that it was up to me to convince
Him to come down and do something. Almost as if God had
unlimited power but had to be convinced to unleash it.

Then I stumbled onto a passage that changed my whole
perspective: "For the eyes of the LORD run to and fro

throughout the whole earth, to show Himself strong on behalf of those whose heart is loyal to Him" (2 Chronicles 16:9).

God wants very much to work in our lives, on earth, far more than we want Him to work in our lives! He constantly scans, east to west, north to south, seeking loyal hearts. Why? In order to show Himself strong by working in our lives.

You can rest assured that it's God's desire to release His hand of power. And you can be confident that He wants to do it through you. Are you ready?

CHAPTER TEN

THE HAND OF GOD:
LIVING IT OUT

Your Dream lies in the direction of an overwhelming obstacle.
If you go toward it today, you will bring God honor.
And you will experience a life marked by miracles
as God intervenes on your behalf.[1]

THE DREAM GIVER

On September 11, 2001, Barbara watched in shock as the twin towers of the World Trade Center were erased from the New York skyline. From the opposite side of the continent, she felt far away and helpless. God began placing a burden on Barbara's heart for the families of the victims.

She prayed, asking God to comfort the brokenhearted. Immediately, the book she had written, *A Passage Through Grief,* came to mind. She had seen firsthand the healing and hope the book offered to hurting people. And hope was exactly what the people of New York were needing right now.

Unfortunately, her book had just gone out of print.

Barbara continued to pray, and before the day was over, she was sure God was telling her to give ten thousand copies of *A Passage Through Grief* to the victims' families in New York.

It was a task that only the hand of God could accomplish.

As soon as possible, she approached her pastor and shared her wild scheme.

He thought of another wrinkle. "How will you distribute the books once they get to New York?"

Barbara remained confident. "If God is powerful enough to get them printed and to New York, He'll see that they go where they're most needed."

The next morning Barbara called her publisher and told them her vision. They agreed to print the books at an estimated cost of $30,000.

She mentally inventoried her personal assets. If she used the small inheritance left by her mother and sold her beloved motor home—in which she enjoyed traveling the country—she could almost cover the cost.

Meanwhile, her pastor wrote e-mails to two professional counselors he knew in New York and asked if they would be willing to help with distribution. The next day he received affirmative replies—but from completely different people.

Upon investigation, he discovered that he had mistakenly sent his plea to every church throughout his denomination! As the day progressed, he received inquiries and messages of encouragement from all over America.

As he later said to Barbara, "God uses human mistakes. But He never makes mistakes."

The next piece fell into place when Barbara's publisher

decided to charge her only $8,350. But the order had to be prepaid.

She charged the order to her credit cards, trusting that God would reimburse her. Over the next few days, the full amount came pouring in from contributors throughout the country.

As for the question of distribution, a pastor in New Jersey—whose church was located only fifteen miles from the World Trade Center—had received one of Barbara's pastor's "stray" e-mails. He wrote, asking to have the books shipped directly to him. He knew exactly how to get them into the right hands.

On October 29, ten thousand books, paid in full, were shipped to the East Coast and put into the hands of hurting people via several churches and the Salvation Army.[2]

PRACTICAL STEPS TO POWER

Barbara's story illustrates the kind of lifestyle through which the hand of God will work—a lifestyle of *proactive dependency* on God. Barbara didn't just sit back and wait to see what God would do; she actively pursued His will in response to the need. But at no point was she running out ahead of God, trying to do it on her own. She remained prayerfully dependent on Him the whole way.

God honored Barbara's faith, obedience, and trust.

Jesus described the life of fruitful faith this way:

> "Abide in Me, and I in you. As the branch cannot bear fruit of itself, unless it abides in the vine, neither can you, unless you abide in Me. I am the vine, you are the

branches. He who abides in Me, and I in him, bears much fruit; for without Me you can do nothing."

JOHN 15:4–5

As you abide in Christ—that is, as you spend time deepening your relationship with Him—you can expect your faith to grow.

I encourage you to pray continually for new vision for the power of God's hand, just as Paul prayed that his first-century friends would know "the exceeding greatness of His power toward us who believe, according to the working of His mighty power which He worked in Christ when He raised Him from the dead and seated Him at His right hand in the heavenly places" (Ephesians 1:19–20).

This very same power that conquered death is available to you. God knows no limitations. He is "able to do exceedingly abundantly above all that we ask or think, according to the power that works in us" (Ephesians 3:20).

Is this the way you want to live? Do you want to dream great dreams and wake to find that God has answered your prayers beyond even your wildest expectations?

If so, then consider two heart conditions that will help make you a suitable conduit for God's power. The first is *humility*. Peter wrote, "Humble yourselves under the mighty hand of God, that He may exalt you in due time" (1 Peter 5:6). Search your heart for vestiges of pride, and invite the Holy Spirit to help with the process. But don't wait until you *feel* humble. Move out in dependent obedience, expecting God to work, not expecting to do the work by yourself. As you see His hand

The same power that conquered death is available to you.

perform miracles that leave you in awe, you will naturally respond with humble worship.

A second heart condition that will enable you to be used powerfully by God is *focus*. Typically, when we see a situation that needs the hand of God to solve the problem, we ask the question, "What can I do if I work hard and if God blesses my efforts?" Instead, we should constantly ask, "What does God want done?" The difference may seem slight, but it is critical to unleashing the power of God in your life.

As you continue to ask God to enlarge your territory, you will find yourself in situations that seem to stretch far beyond your resources or abilities. The human response to such opportunities is either to avoid them and put them out of our minds or to limit our response based on what we think we can do under the circumstances. When you approach life from this perspective, you will rarely experience the hand of the Lord. In fact, you will seek ways to reduce the initial burden you had—until you feel you can do it.

God's hand rarely intervenes when our hand "owns" the problem.

Let me share how the hand of God intervened one week in the small African nation of Swaziland.

I announced to a gathering there that 122 Dream for Africa volunteers from the U.S. and South Africa were coming to partner with them to plant ten thousand Never Ending Gardens for families who had no food. All in one week—that's all the time we had.

Everyone smiled. This was obviously an impossible goal.

A key Swaziland leader laughed and said that if we could plant one thousand gardens in a week it would be a miracle and he would buy me a steak dinner. With as much confidence as I could muster, I replied, "If we don't plant ten thousand in a week, I will buy *you* a steak."

He smiled and said, "Ah, I like mine medium."

Monday came and I shared with our team that no one had ever done something even remotely like this before, but I believed that we were supposed to plant ten thousand gardens in one week. To keep an accurate count, we would take digital pictures of each garden we planted, with the family standing next to it.

By the end of Monday, we had planted three hundred and were tired.

By the end of Tuesday, we had planted six hundred and were very tired.

By the end of Wednesday, we had planted twelve hundred and were very, very tired.

On Thursday, I asked the team to return early to prepare a new strategy, because unless God directly intervened, there was no way that we could ever reach our goal of ten thousand. A few of us stayed back and prayed and fasted and begged the Lord to show us how. Our teams arrived exhausted and discouraged. We planted eleven hundred more.

Thirty-two hundred planted in four days.

Sixty-eight hundred remained. And we had one day.

Energy was nowhere to be found. No one believed it was possible. My most difficult work didn't involve lifting a shovel but, rather, fighting the fears and doubts in my heart.

All day we pleaded for God to show His hand strong on our behalf and to demonstrate His heart for the hungry. I had no idea how we could do it, but I knew that His hand knew no bounds, and we weren't going to sin with unbelief. If God could feed a couple of million people with manna and water in the desert every day, then this task would not be too difficult for him.

As the sun set on Friday afternoon, I stood at the gate with a little pad in my hand as the volunteers drove in. I asked each person, "How many gardens did you plant today?"

A celebration was held that evening, with speeches from the Minister of Enterprise, the U.S. ambassador to Swaziland, the South African ambassador, and finally, a member of the royal family. But before these dignitaries spoke I was able to announce that we had planted a total of 12,874 gardens!

By the way, I enjoyed my T-bone steak medium-rare.

The primary hindrance to most such goals isn't that there is a lack of territory or opportunity, or that the power of God is lacking, or even that there is a lack of willingness or desire on God's part to make it happen. The primary hindrance is a lack of faith: We look at our resources and think, *I can't*; then we look up to heaven and say, "He won't."

Our goal for the coming year of the Never Ending Gardens project is to plant one million gardens, which will provide immune-boosting vegetables for six to eight million people in six nations. Once again, this vastly expanded "territory" seems overwhelming, impossible, even ridiculous. But is God's arm shortened? Will God provide the people to come and help us?

Recently, I had the privilege of speaking at Shadow Mountain Community Church in California, pastored by my good friend Dr. David Jeremiah. The hand of the Lord moved, and before the end of the evening, hundreds flooded to the front and committed to fill a 747 to fly to Swaziland to plant gardens the following February. Dr. Jeremiah and his wife were the first two to sign up!

We believe that God will raise up a total of ten thousand such volunteers to partner with the wonderful people of Africa to plant a million Never Ending Gardens next year.

WATCHING GOD'S HAND AT WORK

What can you expect to see as God's hand works in your life? You will experience remarkable, even miraculous, direct answers to prayer. No one can predict whether the miracles in your life will be large and dramatic or more subtle and private. But if you keep an expectant watch, God's intervention will be unmistakable. Whether it's the provision of millions for a worthy cause or the firm, gentle shifting of a loved one's heart—God will do before your eyes what you could never have done without His intervention.

Deana jumped in with both feet when the Shepherd's Gate ministry opened a Transition Home in her community. Shepherd's Gate provides housing and vocational training for women who are escaping abusive relationships, poverty, and drug and alcohol addictions. In Deana's new role, she tutored the women's children. And she loved it!

But several years earlier, Deana had been diagnosed with a debilitating disease that progressively attacks the nerves. Some days she suffered painful spasms, and the day's fatigue only aggravated them. To make matters worse, the children were available for tutoring only in the afternoons and evenings—the worst times for Deana's condition.

One day she came home in tears, knowing she was working past her limits, even though she was volunteering just two days a week. The agony and fatigue were more than she could take.

Then Deana began to pray that the Lord would expand her territory in spite of her condition. Only hours had passed before she saw the hand of God beginning to work. She received a call from one of the housemothers at the Transition Home. "Deana, if you wouldn't mind, I'd like to help you with your tutoring duties."

Wow, Lord! she thought. *You certainly didn't waste any time answering my prayers!*

With this newfound support available, Deana informed her supervisor that she would be cutting back to one day a week. Her supervisor then put out a call for more volunteers, and four more people responded within the next few weeks. Deana was soon able to back completely out of the hands-on work of tutoring.

Failure? Anything but.

That's when God flung open the doors for a new and more expanded ministry role for Deana. She began to coordinate and organize the home's entire tutoring program. She trained teachers and even developed some of the children's curriculum. She was able to do this work well within her physical limits. And the children began receiving even more help than before from trained and equipped teachers.[3]

Don't let your inadequacy and limitations diminish your expectations of God's ability to work through you. In fact, success in spite of your own inabilities will only serve to highlight the supernatural power of God.

Deana had feared that she was failing God, but He used her limitations to accomplish even more.

He'll do the same for you.

WHEN THE HAND OF GOD LOOKS LIKE YOURS

Do you truly believe that the power of God is available to you? Do you long to experience the incredible joy and awe of watching heaven open its gates to release the power for you to receive and achieve what you are asking?

Remember, the hand of God is set in motion by the heart of God. When what God wants done is similar to what you are asking Him to do, what do you suppose will happen? He will not ask you to walk further and further out on a limb, only to let it collapse under you. And when He asks you to take a leap of faith and jump into His arms, He will not let you fall and laugh and say, "You fool!"

On the last day of our first garden-planting mission in Swaziland, we met a woman who not only had walked to the edge of the limb but had leaped and literally was midair when we arrived, openly trusting the faithful hand of her God to catch her. Let me tell you what happened.

A small group of our Dream for Africa team was planting in the villages when they came upon a lone mud hut surrounded by dozens of children. Then they noticed lots of little gardens had been dug up around the hut, but nothing appeared to be growing in them.

They discovered that the hut was home to an old grandmother who was taking care of fifty-six orphans. That morning she had told the children to dig lots of gardens. When they asked her why—after all, they had no seeds or money—she told them, "Last night I asked God to send someone to plant gardens for us. We must be ready for them when they come." That same morning the young children dug up the ground in faith, while looking toward heaven for the seeds.

Our team was dumbfounded. Here they were with hundreds of seedlings, arriving in the very place, at the very moment, where one of God's children had begged the hand of God to intervene. And He did! He sent stockbrokers from New York, accountants from Connecticut, teachers from Johannesburg, and housewives from Bryanston, South Africa.

The old woman asked for God's hand and He sent theirs.

The last time I checked, the gardens were producing a great deal of food and the old woman now cares for seventy-six children.

PROTECTION BY GOD

And Jabez called on the God of Israel saying,
"Oh, that You would bless me indeed,
and enlarge my territory,
that Your hand would be with me,
and that You would keep me from evil,
that I may not cause pain!"
So God granted him what he requested.

A SECRET
ADDICTION

by David King

"David, what are you doing up at this hour?" my mom would often scold when she found me glued to the computer.

"I'm just playing, Mom. No big deal," I muttered, never taking my eyes from the screen.

"David, stop playing and look at me." I knew she meant business, so I complied. She said, "Ever since you got into playing these violent games, I've seen Satan gaining influence in your heart. You used to have such a heart for God. But this game has drained the life from you. I feel like I don't even know you anymore."

"Mom, give me a break." I turned back to the computer. I'd heard it all before. "You know it's just a game. It doesn't hurt anybody."

Mom shook her head and went back to bed, leaving me to my bloody cyber-existence.

Since being introduced to this highly interactive PC

game, I had been slowly sucked into its violent fantasy world. I joined an on-line gaming league and practiced every day with my Internet teammates. Before long, my grades were slipping, I let my friendships slide, and I was spending every minute of my free time on the computer. Sometimes I didn't even go to bed. The game was my life.

My youth pastor also noticed my lack of direction. He knew I had once thought of becoming a pastor, and he had been trying to direct my focus back on God. He had given me a copy of *The Prayer of Jabez*, and one day after school I felt strangely drawn to the little book. So instead of going to my computer, I sat down to read.

Before long I came to the statement "The only thing that can break this cycle of abundant living is sin, because sin breaks the flow of God's power."

Suddenly, I knew why God seemed so distant and church so dry and boring. The game was no longer just entertainment; for me it had become an idol, an addiction. The passion I once felt for God had been replaced by my obsession with this mind-numbing game.

I closed the book and got on my knees.

Lord, I prayed, feeling a long-dead spark ignite, *I want to confess this sin of idolatry and ask Your forgiveness. How could I have ever let such a vile thing replace my love for You? I want You to be first in my life again.*

With confession came a sense of peace and freedom. But I knew that true repentance meant action, not just words. I went straight to my computer and deleted every trace of the game from my hard drive.

I realized that I had wasted almost three years of my life—time that could have been spent serving God. But thanks to His intervention, I've taken the first steps toward giving my whole life back to Him.

I've since used my reclaimed time to learn guitar, and I'm in a praise band now. I'm once again pursuing healthy friendships. And best of all, I'm seeking God, asking Him how I can do and be my best for Him.

CHAPTER ELEVEN

THE PRAYER FOR PROTECTION: A CLOSER LOOK

We were redeemed and commissioned for the front lines.
That's why praying to be kept from evil is such a
vital part of the blessed life.[1]

THE PRAYER OF JABEZ

S tand your ground!" Your Commander's orders crackle through the radio receiver.

Just then a missile explodes not far from you, shaking the ground and raining down debris. Casualties have been heavy during the latest stage of the battle, especially among those who didn't use their heads, or who lost contact with High Command. And the desertion rate has been high.

You yourself have sustained a few wounds. You're still battle-worthy, but morale is declining. Your unit is undermanned and ill-equipped to deal with the enemy—an enemy who despises you and is bent on your destruction.

Yet you've made significant headway, regaining ground once unjustly claimed by your adversary. He wants it back, and he's using every resource at his disposal to bring you down.

"Sir," you shout into your radio, "we need air support and reinforcements. Now!"

"I thought you might ask," comes the reply. "They should be at your location right about... now."

As you peek over the edge of your foxhole, exhausted relief floods through you. Rank upon rank of armored tanks rumble up to and past your position. Overhead come roaring hundreds of bomb-laden planes. In the face of such overwhelming force, the enemy abandons his fortifications and flees for his life.

A short time later you emerge safely from the trenches. You scan the war-ravaged landscape. Here and there your comrades appear and begin to rally together. A good number remain, but you know there should be many more.

Nonetheless, your spirits are lifted. The Army of Light has once again experienced victory where defeat seemed inevitable. Together you advance to bring freedom to one more town living in darkness.

Many of God's people rise to the challenge to take new territory, only to find themselves under spiritual—sometimes even physical—attack. Because of this, many turn back from pursuing the life exemplified by Jabez.

But what is this life—this gift from the Dream Giver—all about?

New territory is the reason we are here. Your orders are recorded in Matthew 28:18–20. Jesus' commission to go into the whole world and introduce everyone to life in Him wasn't a suggestion, but a command!

And whatever the Lord commands, He always makes possible. If He wants us to walk into battle, then as we obey He is faithful to protect us.

These next few chapters are intended to strengthen your defenses, that you might faithfully and successfully advance, taking new ground for God.

JABEZ'S FINAL REQUEST

"Keep me from evil, that I may not cause pain!" (1 Chronicles 4:10) is the concluding request of Jabez. But what did Jabez mean by this?

In this passage, the word *evil* is the same Hebrew word used in Genesis 6:5 to describe the world before God unleashed the great Flood. Here, it is translated as *wickedness*: "Then the LORD saw that the wickedness of man was great in the earth, and that every intent of the thoughts of his heart was only evil continually."

The same Hebrew word can also, in some contexts, be translated as *pain*. That's why some English translations read, "Keep me from pain." Neither translation is incorrect, but the majority of usages in the Bible are translated as *evil*, not *pain*.

Although *pain* would be an interesting play on the name Jabez (which means "pain"), I believe that Jabez was primarily asking for protection from all types of evil. When Jabez prayed, "Keep me," he was asking that God would act to *protect.*

Jabez even reveals his motive for not wanting evil in his life: "That I may not cause pain." This can also be properly translated *that it may not pain me or grieve me*. The Hebrew grammar used here can be interpreted to mean causing pain to another or to oneself. When we participate in evil, we cause pain and grief both to ourselves and to others, including God.

So we hear Jabez asking God, *Please protect me from doing evil, which would only cause heartbreak for You, for others, and for me.*

WHAT IT MEANS TO PRAY FOR PROTECTION

Let's put Jabez's prayer for protection into the broader context of the Bible, so we are able to understand it more clearly.

1. The prayer is for protection not only from suffering, but also from sin. Is it wrong to ask God to minimize our suffering? Absolutely not. But while God cares about the pain we experience, He is even more concerned for the condition of our relationship with Him. He knows that sin causes far more harm than physical pain or hardship. We pray most effectively when we recognize this, too.

2. The prayer is for protection not only from sin, but also from Satan. As we'll discuss later, there are multiple sources of temptation. But one significant source is the real, living being named Satan and his hordes of fallen angels. If we pray about evil as though it were a completely impersonal influence, we are likely to let down our guard against the malevolent beings who seek our personal downfall.

3. The prayer is for protection not only for the future, but also for the present. Praying about evil keeps you alert to the spiritual battle that rages around you and within you. One of Satan's favorite tricks is to create a false sense of security so that we might drop our defenses.

4. *Refraining from evil is accomplished not only by you, but by God's intervention.* You are asking God to act on your behalf, not merely to send you His best wishes as you fight the battle. The Bible reveals two primary ways to deal with temptation: First, actively resist temptation yourself; second, regularly request that God protect you from it.

EVEN THOUGH HE KNOWS

People are often confused as to how to deal with temptation and sin. Some recognize that temptation is something to avoid or resist, but then their theology takes a left turn where the truth has turned right.

For example, let's say they start with the doctrine of God's omniscience, that God knows everything. *If that's true,* they reason, *then certainly God knows how I will be tempted. And if God doesn't want me to sin, then why can't I assume that He'll simply protect me, whether I ask Him to or not?*

This is...

PROTECTION MISCONCEPTION #1:
*God knows when I am tempted,
so prayer isn't necessary.*

The fact is, praying for protection will greatly affect whether or not you *are* tempted.

One day Jesus' disciples asked Him for praying lessons. They had seen Him pray and observed the results in His life, and they wanted to learn to do the same. In answer, Jesus modeled a simple prayer, which we call the Lord's Prayer. It's very short, perhaps because Jesus wanted to help us focus on those requests that are most important. One of these few requests was, "Do not lead us into temptation, but deliver us from the evil one" (Luke 11:4).

In other words, Jesus taught that one of the indispensable components of a vital prayer life is the request to "keep me from evil." Again, Jesus Himself affirms the concepts voiced in Jabez's prayer.

Later, on the evening before His crucifixion, Jesus went with His disciples to the Garden of Gethsemane to pray. The stress of anticipating the following day's events took a severe toll on him, and Jesus sought comfort from His Father. He also needed the support and prayers of His best friends. But when He found them sleeping, rather than standing with Him, He voiced His disappointment: "What? Could you not watch with Me one hour? Watch and *pray, lest you enter into temptation*" (Matthew 26:40–41). This passage clearly teaches us to both watch and pray, and it directly links our prayers to the temptation we may or may not face.

Did you notice the strategy Jesus taught in both of these passages? *Do not lead us into temptation. Pray, lest you enter into temptation.* The best way to keep from sinning is to avoid temptation altogether! Today, did you ask God to protect you from temptation? If not, perhaps you faced many more temptations than you would have had you prayed as Jesus taught.

Did you ask God to protect you from temptation today?

This is the only request of the Jabez prayer that is difficult to objectively prove that God answered. Why? Because sometimes God steers you away from a temptation and you never even know it. You won't always see His protection in action. Praying for protection is an act of faith. You can trust that He hears and grants your request because you are praying in keeping with His will. He doesn't want you to sin.

On the other hand, some temptation in life is unavoidable. At this point, simply keep in mind that we must watch and pray to *avoid* temptation as much as possible. That's our best defense against evil.

EVEN THOUGH HE HEARS

Others take a different approach to the whole temptation problem. They agree that it's good to avoid temptation, and they even believe that prayer for God's protection is essential. But they figure, *How often do I have to pray, really? Once a week ought to do the trick. God won't forget what I asked Him on Sunday while at church. After all, I don't want to bore Him with asking over and over again.*

This leads to...

> PROTECTION MISCONCEPTION #2:
> *I don't have to watch out for temptation.*
> *I'm prayed up.*

But merely praying for protection doesn't guarantee you will not sin. We must keep firmly in mind God's warning: "Let him who thinks he stands take heed lest he fall" (1 Corinthians 10:12).

Just as the boxer can't afford to lower his guard for one second, lest his opponent exploit the opening and deliver a knockout punch, so also we must remain in constant dependence on God, that He might continually protect us against our relentless adversary. That's one reason Paul instructed us, "Pray without ceasing" (1 Thessalonians 5:17).

EVEN THOUGH YOU ARE SERVING

I've often told this story from my freshman year of graduate school, and it bears repeating here. One day six or seven of us remained after class to talk to one of our favorite professors, Dr. Howard Hendricks. During the conversation, my friend standing in front of me said, "You know, Dr. Hendricks, when I first came to this seminary, my life was full of temptations and struggles. But now after studying Greek, Hebrew, and theology, my life is smooth as glass."

And I remember thinking, *Wow! I'd give my right arm to have a life like that.* I slowly shrank back a few steps. *Maybe it's better if I don't bother him with any questions.*

But Dr. Hendricks suddenly had a look of alarm. "Young man," he said to my friend, "that's the worst thing you could possibly have said to me. Before you came here, at least you were in the battle. But now you've shown me that the enemy doesn't even think you're worth harassing."

My embarrassed friend had succumbed to...

PROTECTION MISCONCEPTION #3:
God especially protects me when I'm serving Him.

The assumption is that when we're serving God, He automatically puts a circle of warrior angels or a "hedge of protection" around us to guard us from temptation. *So as long as I'm ministering,* we think, *I don't need to worry about sin.*

The truth is, praying for protection is most critical when you're actively serving God!

You don't shed your human tendency toward sin when you step into a pulpit or share a meal with a lonely person or tell a friend about God. Often the greatest temptations and difficulties come to the person who is living the Jabez life. You're taking away the enemy's territory, so he is likely to target you as a threat.

Praying for protection is most critical when you're actively serving God.

Keep in mind that God never promised to keep all temptation away from you. In particular, watch carefully for temptation at two specific times: (1) just before a significant effort in God's service and (2) just after such an effort, when you're physically and spiritually exhausted. During these times, keep your heart especially close to God and frequently ask for protection from temptation.

A wise course of action is to preempt temptation before it has a chance to strike, by implementing practical safeguards against the sins you have the hardest time resisting. Set up an accountability phone call. Travel a route that avoids moral snares. Remove from your life any temptations that you know are likely to lead you into stronger temptation and sin.

A friend shared with me one evening that he couldn't seem to break his habit of watching pornography on one particular cable television station. I asked him how seriously he desired to break free from this damaging habit. He quickly responded, "I'm very, very anxious for a victory."

I smiled and told him that there was a surefire solution that could erase the problem instantly. He sat up in his chair, with a thrilled look. I don't know what he was expecting, but it wasn't what he heard: "Just cancel your cable contract, and the temptation will instantly disappear!"

With utter shock, he said, "I can't do that! There are too many great movies."

I smiled and responded, "Well, I guess we've just determined your true level of desire to be free from pornography."

Two weeks went by, and we bumped into each other at a nearby store. He walked up, smiled, and said, "I canceled it that night and I've been free ever since!"

THE DANGER IS REAL

Jesus never fostered any illusions among His followers. It's a dangerous world, He said, but God is greater than anything in the world (see John 16:20–22, 33). The stakes are high, but they're worth every effort to win the battle against sin.

For the sake of everyone you love—for the love of your heavenly Father—stay continually close within the haven of His protective embrace. And whatever you do, pray the prayer of protection as modeled by Jesus and Jabez each day.

CHAPTER TWELVE

THE PRAYER FOR PROTECTION: GOING DEEPER

No temptation has overtaken you except such as is common to man; but God is faithful, who will not allow you to be tempted beyond what you are able, but with the temptation will also make the way of escape, that you may be able to bear it.

1 CORINTHIANS 10:13

*T*he temptation was unexpected and intense, and I was totally unprepared.

It happened in Maryland after I had taught the Walk Thru the Old Testament seminar all day at the church of one of my seminary friends. The church was packed out, the audience electric, and I poured my heart into the teaching. We had a tremendous time, and as I walked to my hotel room I felt fulfilled. I had given everything I could in ministry, and

I had barely enough energy to make it down the hallway.

I dropped my large case of overhead transparencies on the floor, sat on the edge of the bed, and started to remove my tie. A hot shower was going to feel great. Then came a soft knock on the door. I couldn't imagine who it would be. Perhaps it was my friend from the church returning something I had forgotten.

Without thinking, I opened the door and there stood a very attractive young woman. She looked right into my eyes and said, "Let's have some fun tonight—just you and me." She lowered her voice and said, "No one will ever know."

I remember struggling to find the words to reply. Then the thought rushed in: *Maybe you should invite her in and witness to her.*

My heart pumped so loud and so fast, I began to sweat. I knew that I was in big-time danger and had better flee instantly. The words barely escaping my dry throat, I replied, "No thanks." And slammed the door.

I sat down on the edge of my bed, trembling. Literally. This temptation came after me suddenly and powerfully, without any warning whatsoever. Although less than a minute passed between us, it felt like an eternity.

How thankful I am to the Lord for His sustaining hand in the sight of a temptation that could have ruined my marriage and ministry. Almost thirty years have passed since that day, but I'm forever thankful for the power of the prayer, "Keep me from evil!"

THE FLESH AND THE WORLD

The flesh is the first of three sources of temptation that Scripture warns us about. In the Bible *the flesh* is described simply as your own desire to sin. According to Galatians 5:19–20, "The works of the flesh are evident, which are: adultery, fornication, uncleanness, lewdness, idolatry, sorcery, hatred..."

The list continues on for most of two more verses.

Keep in mind that Paul wrote that passage to believers! No matter how long you've walked with God, your flesh will always be with you this side of death, and will always fight against what God wants. Paul tells us that the Spirit wars against the flesh, and that these things are contrary to one another (see Galatians 5:17).

Our flesh never improves; it never becomes more like the Spirit over time. That's why we are told to crucify our flesh and walk instead by means of the Spirit.

Well then, you might ask, if the flesh never gets any better, how is it possible for a person to become more like Christ? Only by the grace and power of God. As you grow in dependence on the Holy Spirit, He overcomes the flesh so that your life is free to bear the fruit of the Spirit (see Galatians 5:22–23). Paul called this *walking in the Spirit,* and every time you pray "keep me from the temptation of my flesh," you are choosing to depend on the Spirit.

Your flesh will always fight against what God wants. Choose instead to depend on the Spirit.

A second source of temptation is *the world.* The apostle John wrote, "Do not love the world or the things in the world. If anyone loves the world, the love of the Father is not in him. For all that is in the world—the lust of the flesh, the lust of the eyes, and the pride of life—is not of the Father but is of the world" (1 John 2:15–16).

The world is a system of values and beliefs, many of which

war against the love of God, because the system is deceitfully influenced and controlled by our enemy (see Ephesians 2:2; 6:12). That's why Paul warns us in Romans 12:2 not to let the world squeeze us into its mold.

Yet we are constantly bombarded with the world's messages—in schools, in the media, in business. Advertisements try to create discontentment, enticing us to become obsessively greedy. The business world encourages us to advance our own interests, even if it requires walking all over other people.

But God says, *Shift your affections from things of the world to things of eternity—to lasting wealth that makes this world's attractions seem worthless.* As the apostle said, love of the world and love for God cannot coexist in the same moment.

How do you guard your heart for God against the world? Only by continually giving God supremacy in all areas of your life. Therefore, habitually pray, "Keep me from the world's temptation."

THE FORCES OF DARKNESS

The third source of temptation is also external. But while the world is an impersonal system, this one is maliciously personal. He is called *the devil,* or *Satan.* And he has an army of fallen angels—frequently called demons in the Gospels— working for him.

Paul described our struggle with Satan and his forces this way:

> For we do not wrestle against flesh and blood, but against principalities, against powers, against the rulers of the darkness of this age, against spiritual hosts

of wickedness in the heavenly places. Therefore take up the whole armor of God, that you may be able to withstand in the evil day, and having done all, to stand.

EPHESIANS 6:12–13

Many people—even many Christians—don't believe Satan is a real entity. But the Bible tells us that Satan was once named Lucifer and was the strongest and most brilliant of all the angels (see Isaiah 14:12–15). He rebelled against God and suffered an eternal defeat. So now he hates God and wants to hurt Him by hurting those who serve Him. He wants to keep as many people as possible in spiritual darkness, or at least in bondage to sin, so they cannot serve God.

If you live your whole life within your comfort zone, you're not much of a threat to the enemy. But when you stretch yourself for God beyond what feels safe, when you anticipate fear and choose not to run from it, when in God's strength you walk right past your border bullies, and when the hand of God enables you to take new territory—that's when Satan begins to oppose you most actively.

Please understand, I'm not saying that Satan is lying in wait under every rock and behind every bush. He is not the cause of every bad thing that happens to you, because there are other sources of temptation and difficulty. Obsessing on Satan is just as dangerous as ignoring him.

But he is real. He is vicious. And you should expect his opposition when you live the Jabez life.

However, he need not prevail over you, "because He who is in you is greater than he who is in the world" (1 John 4:4). Satan is a limited being—one of God's creations. That's why Paul tells us to be strong in the Lord, put on the equipment He has provided for battle, and ensure victory by drawing upon

God's power and protection through prayer (see Ephesians 6:13–18).

James wrote, "Submit to God. Resist the devil and he will flee from you" (James 4:7). When you pray, you are voicing to God your dependence on Him. And when you ask, "Keep me from temptation," and you exercise Spirit-empowered self-control, you are resisting Satan by bringing to bear the might of God against your enemy.

THE COST OF SIN

God has placed us in a cause-and-effect world. And He warns us that every sin has a consequence. Sometimes the consequence comes as a natural result of our actions; other times God steps in directly and disciplines His child.

Some sins are greater than others (God describes some sins as "more abominable" than others in Ezekiel 16:52) and carry heavier consequences, especially for those who have lived many years for God or hold an office of spiritual authority—these God holds to a higher level of accountability (see James 3:1; 1 Timothy 3:2–12).

Look at what happened in the life of King David when, in a moment of selfish independence, he committed adultery with Bathsheba. After she became pregnant by him, David murdered her husband in an attempt to cover his sin. But God had entrusted David with a high responsibility—the civil and spiritual leadership of His people. And so God brought severe consequences upon David's house:

"Now therefore, the sword shall never depart from your house, because you have despised Me, and have taken the wife of Uriah the Hittite to be your wife...

"Behold, I will raise up adversity against you from your own house; and I will take your wives before your eyes and give them to your neighbor, and he shall lie with your wives in the sight of this sun...

"Because by this deed you have given great occasion to the enemies of the LORD to blaspheme, the child also who is born to you shall surely die."

2 SAMUEL 12:10–11, 14

The story brings home with startling clarity the seriousness of sin, especially major or ongoing sin. And it also illustrates the fact that the consequences of our sin often result in severe trauma to others.

God warns us about the potential consequences of sin so that we might seek His continual protection from evil.

ALWAYS A WAY OUT

While avoidance of temptation is the best way to keep from sinning, what will God do for you when you find yourself face-to-face with temptation? Sometimes the lure can seem overpowering, relentless, irresistible. Sin may feel inevitable.

God says differently. Listen to His promise:

No temptation has overtaken you except such as is common to man; but God is faithful, who will not allow you to be tempted beyond what you are able, but with the temptation will also make the way of escape, that you may be able to bear it.

1 CORINTHIANS 10:13

You need never give up hope of holiness. When you find yourself in the midst of any kind of temptation, God says, *I'm right there in it with you, because I don't want you to sin.*

In this verse, the Lord promises to do two things. First, He will limit the potency of the temptation—that is, He will not allow you "to be tempted beyond what you are able" to withstand. If your flesh, the world, or the devil targets you with an overwhelming temptation, God puts up His sovereign filter and allows only those life experiences to occur that are within your Spirit-empowered ability to bear.

And second, when it seems you're stuck in a canyon, with insurmountable cliffs on all sides, God promises to make a way of escape. In the midst of any temptation cry out, "Lord, where's the exit door?" and He will show you the way out.

DANGERS WE ARE TO PRAY AGAINST

Who can number the many temptations you might face in your lifetime, against which you must ask God for protection? I have selected for discussion here four types of temptation that may present a special danger to the man or woman who is advancing into a lifestyle of Jabez-type praying and living.

First, pray for protection from the temptation of *pride*. James 4:6 says, "God resists the proud, but gives grace to the humble."

When God works through your life, it's a team effort— God's power working through your willing heart, your wisdom, and your effort. It's appropriate for you to accept an expression of appreciation for your service, but never for God's power. Sometimes, as God's hand begins to perform greater and greater works through you, pride can lure you subtly into believing that you deserve the credit that belongs only to the Lord.

This happened to Moses, and it's the reason he was prohibited from entering into the Promised Land. One day when the thirsty people could find no water, God instructed Moses to speak to a rock, promising him that it would produce water. Instead of speaking to the rock, however, Moses struck it with his staff, as he had been told to do on a previous occasion. The water gushed forth from the rock, and the people's thirst was quenched (see Numbers 20:2–12).

But God told Moses that because of that one act, he would die in the desert. For what? For hitting a rock instead of speaking to it? Doesn't seem quite fair—until you look closer at what actually happened.

Notice in verse 10 the words Moses spoke just before he struck the rock: "Hear now, you rebels! *Must we bring water for you out of this rock?*" (emphasis added). Did you see the pronoun Moses used? *We*. Moses had crossed the line and taken for himself some of the glory that was God's alone. He put himself in the spotlight that belonged only to God. Pride, not anger, was the sin for which Moses was disciplined. God's judgment: "Because you did not believe Me, to hallow Me in the eyes of the children of Israel, therefore you shall not bring this assembly into the land which I have given them."

Regularly ask God to guard your heart from pride.

WHEN A GOOD THING TURNS BAD

Second, pray for protection from the temptation of *power*. Power is not necessarily the same as authority, although it often accompanies a person's position. You might derive power from reputation or fame, from connections, from money, or from skills and education. Or it may come with the powerful influence of God's hand working in your life.

From studying the New Testament, it appears that power was a frequent temptation for the disciples. On more than one occasion they argued over who among them was the greatest (see Mark 9:33–34; 10:35–37; Luke 22:24). Jesus even found it necessary to teach them not to "lord it over" one another (Mark 10:42–45).

In any of your relationships—especially those in which you exercise influence on others—watch the way you treat people. Listen to your tone of voice. Pay attention to whether you become pushy and how well you listen to others' opinions. Be careful how you use your authority. God gave it to you (see Romans 13:1) and He can take it right back. Pray that He would guard you from the subtle temptation of power.

Third, pray for protection from the temptation of *possessions.* Money itself is not evil, as it is only a piece of paper or metal. But money is a tool that can be used either for good or for evil. The difference is in our attitude and actions. As you read the following passage, watch for the words that describe a dangerous attitude toward wealth:

> Those who desire to be rich fall into temptation and a snare, and into many foolish and harmful lusts which drown men in destruction and perdition. For the love of money is a root of all kinds of evil, for which some have strayed from the faith in their greediness, and pierced themselves through with many sorrows.
>
> 1 TIMOTHY 6:9–10

Desire to be rich. Lusts. Love of money. Greediness. These are the sins of the heart from which we need God's protection. What a tragic and potent word picture describing those who fall victim to these sins: *They pierce themselves through with many sorrows!*

After giving the keynote address at a national convention, my wife and I were approached by an intense pastor who invited me to speak at his church. "My people need this message. You must come and preach for me," he said.

I smiled and gave him my usual response—"Write me a letter"—because I need time to pray and consider each opportunity. But the pastor persisted, and each time I told him to write me, the honorarium climbed higher.

Finally he said, "We'll pay you an honorarium of $5,000 and give you and your wife a week's vacation in Hawaii."

I stopped him and said, "Sir, do you know what you're saying? You're assuming that if you pay me enough, I'll come. But if that were my true motive, would you *want* me to come? Please, *don't* write me a letter."

Several months later I learned that, sadly, the man had been imprisoned for financial impropriety. He had tried to motivate with the very thing that motivated him; he tempted me with an inappropriate approach to money.

In your heart, keep money in its place—as a tool for eternity, not an idol.

Pray that God would guard you from greed regarding possessions.

THE DANGER BEHIND THE DRIVE

And fourth, pray for protection from the temptation of sinful *pleasure.* It's important to understand that the experience of pleasure is a wonderful gift from God Himself "who gives us richly all things to enjoy" (1 Timothy 6:17). When you think about it, most temptations are normal, God-given desires—which are good, in and of themselves—expressed in a manner that is inappropriate.

Take our sexuality. According to Hebrews 13:4, sexual pleasure within marriage is "honorable." But when we permit our desire for sexual pleasure to take us beyond the clear biblical boundaries, we succumb to the temptation of sexual immorality. In 1 Corinthians 6:18, Paul warns us to "flee sexual immorality."

Why do I include this in my short list of temptations? Because in our day, sexual sin may well cause the greatest number of failures among believers and Christian leaders.

The more God is using you, the more you must pray that He will guard your heart against lust. Attacks can happen to anyone, and they're never announced ahead of time. So you must remain fortified under God's protection at all times.

In Genesis 39:7–12, when Potiphar's wife tried to seduce Joseph, why was he able to say no and flee without hesitation? Because of his close walk with the God who protects us from evil.

From this point on, and for the rest of your life, I encourage you to carefully follow Joseph's example. Never lose awareness that you cannot win the spiritual battle alone. Stay close to God and you will finish well.

WILL YOU SHAKE ON IT?

Before closing this chapter, I would like to invite you to join the ranks of those who have entered into the Ritual of the Handshake.

Many years ago, when I discovered that sexual temptations were so strong and prevalent, especially for those who traveled from home frequently (like Walk Thru the Bible instructors), I sought for an approach that would strengthen all of us.

At a faculty training conference in the early 1980s, I instituted what became affectionately known as the Ritual of the Handshake. Before we departed, I asked the faculty to join me in committing to one another and to the Lord that we would remain sexually pure until we gathered again in a year. "If you are willing," I said, "then take a public stand and come up here and shake my hand." The Ritual of the Handshake proved a significant moment for us all.

I didn't know how significant, however, until one night years later when one of our most outstanding teachers shared with a few of us and our wives an incident that happened as he traveled to teach one weekend. This is what he told us:

Attacks can happen to anyone, anytime. Remain fortified under God's protection

"I was flying back from a little town in the Midwest after teaching, when a massive snowstorm struck the area. We had flown into a major airport in a little prop plane, but the snow was coming down so hard that they closed the airport for the night.

"There were only about eight of us in our party of weary travelers who were invited to climb into a van to drive to a nearby hotel to spend the night. I noticed a very attractive woman, who was traveling alone like I was, but tried not to make any eye contact. When they opened the door of the van, I headed to the back row next to the window. The woman climbed in next, and sat right against my side. Tight. There was no place to go, so I tried to look out the window.

"She kept talking to me in personal tones as we drove to the hotel. It was obvious that she wanted some company that night. *Not with me!* I thought. When we got out of the van at the hotel, I immediately went to the restroom so she wouldn't know where my room was. I looked around the corner and saw that no one was there so I went up to check in.

"As I took my key, she appeared from a corner of the lobby and started walking with me the whole way down to my room. Halfway down the hall, she took my arm and pressed up against me. I was carrying suitcases in both hands and didn't know what to do.

"She started telling me how lonely she was, that her husband was abusive, that they had been separated for many months, and that she desperately needed some friendship for the night."

My friend stopped for a moment and looked at his wife, who already knew the story. He took a deep breath and continued.

"She was a beautiful woman. I stopped at my door and told her I was married and didn't want to be unfaithful to my spouse. As soon as I got into my room, I locked and bolted my door.

"The hotel didn't have room service and I hadn't eaten for eight hours, but I didn't want to run into her. It was past 9:00 P.M. before I ventured out of my room to get something to eat at the restaurant. Hardly anyone was there, and I breathed a bit easier because she wasn't anywhere to be seen. I slipped into a booth and started looking over the menu. Before I knew what was happening, she slid right in next to me and took my arm as she looked over the menu with me.

"I didn't know what to do, but the longer she talked and the longer I looked into her eyes, the more I weakened. My resolve melted as each moment passed. Soon I was giving myself all the reasons why I needed to be with her that night."

He choked up for a moment and looked down at the table.

"I never thought this could possibly happen to me. But it did. Before I knew it, we were standing together right outside my room.

"I'm ashamed to admit it, but at that moment I didn't care about my ministry. I didn't care about my marriage. I didn't even care what would happen to our children at that moment. Nothing else mattered; I just wanted her.

"As I reached out my hand and put the key into the lock, a vivid picture struck me. It was of the night when I shook your hand, Bruce, at the Ritual of the Handshake. The memory of that commitment suddenly brought me strength I know I didn't have. Somehow, the Lord helped me to say no as I opened the door, ran in, and sat trembling in the corner."

With tears in his eyes, he took his wife's hand and said, "I can't thank you enough. The Ritual of the Handshake saved my ministry, my marriage, my children, and even my life!"

What about you? Will you join with me in affirming your commitment to remain strong in the face of sexual temptation? Will you shake my hand in your mind's eye? Perhaps when our paths cross, you can shake my hand in person and acknowledge, "I'm a member of the Ritual of the Handshake."

Until then, pray like Jabez: "Oh Lord, keep me from evil, that I may not cause pain!"

PUBLISHER'S NOTE: You can learn more about how to overcome sexual temptations in Bruce Wilkinson's *Set Apart: Discovering Personal Victory Through Holiness* (Multnomah Publishers, 2003).

CHAPTER THIRTEEN

THE PRAYER FOR PROTECTION: LIVING IT OUT

Lord, keep me from making the mistakes I'm most prone to
when temptation comes. I confess that what I think is
necessary, smart, or personally beneficial is so often only the
beautiful wrapping on sin. So please, keep evil far from me![1]

*O*utwardly, Steven managed to keep up a happy
demeanor, fooling a lot of people. But inwardly he was
constantly tormented by a paradoxical blend of guilt and
resentment. Guilt, because he thought he had killed his father.
Resentment, because he blamed God for what had happened.

Two years earlier, Steven had waited at the hospital while
his father underwent a bone marrow transplant. When a
complication arose and additional surgery was required,

Steven was forced to make a pressured decision regarding the type of pain relief to be used. Concerned for his father's comfort, he chose the general anesthetic rather than a local.

While he paced the corridors, Steven prayed, *Let everything be okay, God. Dad's only fifty-one. Don't take him now.*

But Steven's father unexpectedly reacted adversely to the anesthetic and died in surgery.

Steven walked away from God. For two years he buried himself in work and materialism, wandering through life in spiritual darkness. His family suffered with him, though he denied that anything was wrong.

But he couldn't fool his mother. One day he stopped by her house for a visit. She brushed aside his attempt at small talk and got right to the point. "Steven, I'm worried about you. It's almost as if someone has stolen your soul," she said.

The walls he had built up inside suddenly crumbled, and for the next hour he poured out his heart. He told his mother about his constant guilt and his decision to reject God— about all the pain of the past two years.

Before he left, she advised him, "Steven, you have to trust God. Whatever He's calling you to do, you can't do it alone. You need Him now more than ever." And she handed him a little book called *The Prayer of Jabez.*

Next day, Steven read the book and, for the first time since his father's death, began to believe that God had not forgotten him. He learned that God had a plan for his life—a plan that Steven would not always understand, but a good plan nonetheless. He realized that he needed to depend on God. But he couldn't take such a humbling step without God's help protecting him from his pride—the downside of his take-charge personality.

Steven also needed supernatural defense against the false messages of guilt and blame—messages perhaps originating in his own mind, but certainly also reinforced by the accuser. So he began to pray for protection from evil.

Over time the pain was displaced by peace. Steven came to terms with his father's death and began to anticipate seeing him again in heaven. He found a refreshing sense of purpose as he took his first steps into the new territory God had designated just for him.[2]

STEPS FOR SPIRITUAL DEFENSE

Each of us, like Steven, will encounter his or her own uniquely customized set of temptations. But because God's ultimate goals for all His children are the same—holy character, obedient service, and unhindered communion with Him—the practical steps for protection from evil are similar for all believers. Let's examine four basic steps.

First, *anticipate temptations*, especially as your territory increases. Have you ever wondered why Jesus singled Simon Peter out when, on the night before His crucifixion, He said, "Simon, Simon! Indeed, Satan has asked for you, that he may sift you as wheat" (Luke 22:31)? Satan knew Peter's strategic role as leader of the disciples and soon-to-be leader of the Jewish church. It would fall to Peter, after Jesus' death, to strengthen his brethren, so Jesus prayed especially for Peter's protection from evil.

Peter responded to Jesus' warning with denial: "Lord, I am ready to go with You, both to prison and to death." That's when Jesus predicted that Peter would deny Him three times before the night had ended (vv. 33–34).

Jesus was right. Peter was unprepared when the temptations came (vv. 54–62), and his subsequent remorse might easily have derailed his faith completely, if not for the protective hand of God.

Keep your eyes open. You *will* be tempted.

UNHINDERED FOR SERVICE

Second, *get rid of the one sin that repeatedly defeats you.* The Word of God exhorts us, "Let us lay aside every weight, and *the sin which so easily ensnares us,* and let us run with endurance the race that is set before us" (Hebrews 12:1, emphasis added). Just as a runner can't perform with bulky shoes or clothing entangling his feet and legs, so neither can you fulfill God's purpose in your life if you're enmeshed in sin.

Paul writes, "'Let everyone who names the name of Christ depart from iniquity.' Therefore if anyone cleanses himself... he will be a vessel for honor, sanctified and useful for the Master, prepared for every good work" (2 Timothy 2:19, 21).

You can find complete freedom by "looking unto Jesus, the author and finisher of our faith" (Hebrews 12:2). In His strength, you will be able to lay aside your encumbering sin, and God's hand will work through your life.

Keep me from evil is a prayer for freedom.

You cannot fulfill God's purpose in your life if you're entangled in sin.

Every time I think of this prayer, I remember the time I experienced an immediate, dramatic answer to this powerful request. I had just finished a week of intense ministry at a large college, often counseling late into the night. As I was in the taxi, headed to the airport, I told the Lord, "I'm exhausted spiritually and physically. Please keep all temptations away from me."

When I received my boarding pass to Atlanta, my heart sunk. I had been assigned the middle seat. Not only was it sure to be tight quarters, but I had no idea who might be sitting on either side of me. I had just taken my seat when I heard raucous laughter coming from the front of the plane. Two very heavy men were heading in my direction, laughing a bit too loud. *Oh, no Lord, please, don't...*

One of the men took the window seat, opened his briefcase, and took out a pornographic magazine. The other man took the aisle set, opened his briefcase, and took out a similar graphic magazine.

There was nowhere to go.

I tried to get my courage up to say something, but my reserves had been long used up. So I kept looking at the light above me and prayed, *Lord, I thought we had an agreement. I serve You with all my heart and now look at this. I don't want to sin. Please do me a favor and help—make these men close their magazines.*

Within seconds, one cursed, slammed shut the magazine, and put it in his briefcase. The other did the same. And I started laughing out loud. One of the men asked what I was laughing about and I said, "If I told you, you would never believe me."

Shortly thereafter, I preached on the prayer of Jabez at the First Baptist Church of Atlanta, Georgia, pastored by Dr. Charles Stanley, and I told that story.

A couple of weeks had passed when one of our employees at Walk Thru the Bible stopped me in the hallway with a story I "just had to hear." It turns out her twelve-year-old son was flying to see his grandparents when the man next to him opened a pornographic magazine. He told his Mom, "I figured if God could do it for Dr. Wilkinson, maybe He could do it for me." So he told his mother that he tried to remember the exact words I said and prayed, "Lord, just like You did it to Dr. Wilkinson, would You close the dirty magazine." And God did!

Never underestimate the power of praying, "Keep me from evil." Ask God to keep you away from temptation—even when you are in the middle of it!

STRENGTH TO STAND

Third, *be continually filled with the Spirit's power.* We know that at the point of salvation, God's Spirit comes to live in the believer. But by our choices, we can either hinder or release the Spirit to work through us by His presence and power.

Ephesians 5:18 says, "Do not be drunk with wine, in which is dissipation; but be filled with the Spirit." The Greek grammar used here implies a continual habit of being filled and refilled, over and over. We need to choose to give God's Spirit more control in our lives. That's being filled with the Spirit—a commitment that must be renewed continually.

And fourth, *stand in the power of God's might.* How do you learn to do this? Only by fighting in battle until you experience victory. His might, plus your choice to obey and keep on fighting, always leads to a clear and lasting victory.

Always keep foremost in your thinking that Christ is stronger than anything that will ever come against you. In His power, become His mighty warrior. Every day strap on His armor: truth, righteousness, the gospel of peace, faith, and salvation. And take up His weapons: the Word of God... and prayer (see Ephesians 6:10–18).

Fight! Fight to stand your ground!

And if you grow weary or you're wounded and you fall to one knee, call a friend and say, "I need help! Pray for me!"

God wants you to stand. And He will provide all you need to stand firm.

GET READY FOR FREEDOM!

What will your life be like when you've learned to pray *keep me from evil* with the heart of Jabez? You can be sure that you will become more sensitive to evil and you'll grow in holiness.

Peter learned the hard way the power of temptation and evil, as well as the greater power of God. Later in his life he would instruct Christians, "Gird up the loins of your mind, be sober...as obedient children, not conforming yourselves to the former lusts, *as in your ignorance;* but as He who called you is holy, you also be holy in all your conduct, because it is written, 'Be holy, for I am holy'" (1 Peter 1:13–16, emphasis added).

In the past you were ignorant—you didn't know. But praying for protection heightens your awareness of right and wrong. One of the tools God uses to answer your prayer is your own increasing discernment.

As humans, we have an amazing capacity *not* to discern evil when we see it. Or even when we're right in the middle of it! Regularly praying that God would keep you from evil will heighten your awareness of evil and temptation like you've never known.

By your choices, you can either hinder or release the Spirit to work in your life.

A woman named Virginia grew up dabbling in the occult from childhood. Her mom even encouraged it, not realizing how dangerous it was. Virginia thought it was fun to hold séances and play with Ouija boards with her friends. But the fun faded quickly when apparitions started to appear, doors opened and closed by themselves, and all kinds of evil manifestations occurred.

In spite of her fears, Virginia was unable to let go of witchcraft because it provided a strongly addicting sense of power. She had no idea the degree of evil with which she was involved, even after her boyfriend confronted her.

She covertly continued her occult activities after they were married. But when her first child came along, she realized she needed to reexamine her values. One night she "just happened" to catch a Christian TV program on which the host was interviewing an ex-Satanist. As this man described how the Lord had captured his heart and delivered him from demonic oppression, Virginia's awareness of danger grew, along with her hope of rescue. That night she became a citizen of the kingdom of light.

She started her new life by destroying all the items in her home related to the occult, and to this day, she is extremely sensitive to anything that represents that wicked realm.

Before long, because of her new freedom, God enlarged Virginia's territory by giving her an opportunity to share her amazing story with her church's youth group. She prayed her way out of her comfort zone and past her border bullies, and she shared her testimony at the meeting. Eight kids placed their faith in Christ that night.

A few days later a friend going into the Navy as a chaplain asked for a tape of her testimony to use in his ministry.

Today, Virginia has no idea how many people have been impacted by the story of God's work in her life. But she knows the miracles would never have started if God hadn't awakened her sensitivity to evil and started her on the path to holiness.[3]

THE PROOF IS IN THE DOING

Now, I say time and time again that God can keep you from evil, but you won't *know* it until you start praying for and *experiencing* His protection yourself. When you do, some of your usual temptations will begin to decrease in frequency as God protects you. Meanwhile, other temptations may become more intense, as the enemy turns on the heat.

But you're still safe (see Jude 1:24–25). God will strengthen your self-control, so that you are able to make wiser choices to steer clear of temptation. When you can't avoid it, you'll have strength to walk away or resist. And when sin seems inevitable, you will discover the exit doors God always provides.

Think also of the pain that evil has caused in your past— to you, to people around you, and to God. If you stay close within God's protective embrace, no longer will you cause pain, but joy! Your life will become a source of great blessing to everyone you touch.

And that "Well done!" you're waiting to hear? If you choose to live for holiness in God's strength, I promise you will catch a taste of His pleasure even now, as He smiles on you and your service for Him.

YES, EVEN YOU

I want to address one last scenario that may describe your current situation. By now you may be thinking, *This Jabez life sounds wonderful!* But even as you read this book, you don't believe you could ever live it. Because some sin has you trapped.

Now it's time for us to deal with it honestly.

The truth is that, unless you break the stranglehold of sin, everything in this book will be nothing more than empty words. You'll watch from a distance as others experience abundant blessing, enlarged territory and influence, the ever-available power of God, and protection from evil. But for you it will be nothing more than theory.

I assure you that no matter what has you trapped, or how strong its hold, Jesus Christ's death on the cross has broken both the penalty and the power of your sin. The same power that raised Jesus from the dead is available to lift you up out of your private pit.

If this describes your situation, please seek guidance from a leader in your church or a Christian counselor. They will help you find freedom.

You don't have to go on trapped in sin.

MAKE THE BREAK

Sometimes it takes great courage to make a break with the sin that has you locked in its power. Years ago in the northwestern United States, I spoke at a weekend retreat attended exclusively by men—eight hundred of them. On

Saturday evening, I was asked to confront what the leadership felt was trapping many men in our society: sexual immorality.

At the end of my message I said, "I know that some of you married men are engaged right now in adulterous affairs. And others are having sex before marriage."

The room became quiet. Very quiet.

"There's a phone on that light pole, right outside this building." I pointed through the open side of the rustic building to where a pay phone was visible. "This is your opportunity to break free. Tonight, I'm challenging you to end your sexual immorality. Take a quarter, call the woman with whom you're having the affair, and end it tonight. Tell her how you've hurt her, yourself, your family, and God. Ask her forgiveness and make it clear that you'll never have any contact with her again."

Everyone, it seemed, had stopped breathing.

I continued, "I want you to walk right up this aisle to the front, shake my hand, look me in the eye, tell me you're ending it, and go make the call. For some of you, this is going to be the most difficult call of your life. But by God's grace and your choice, you can and will be set free."

I waited, my heart pounding, and I prayed, *Lord, help these men!*

An eternity passed. Finally a large, husky man stood near the back. The room was so quiet we heard his knees pop. His big boots thudded down the aisle as he held me steadily in his stern gaze. I thought to myself, *This guy is going to punch me out.*

When he reached the spot in front of me, he stopped and said, "I'm a trucker."

I quickly agreed. "Yes, sir, I can see you are."

He said, "I've been having one of those adulterous affairs you've been talking about for nine years. I didn't know God was that much against it, but I can see it now. I'm going to stop it tonight."

Relieved, I reached out to shake his hand. He ignored my hand and instead gave me a big bear hug, lifting me right off the ground. We all watched as he walked out to the phone, his boots crunching through the gravel. When he made the call, we could even hear the quarter hit bottom.

After that, the dam broke and a steady stream of men proceeded to the front, then out to the phone. Later, at two o'clock in the morning, I looked out my cabin window. Men were still standing in line to make their calls.

If God could enable all of these men to make such a difficult and humiliating break from such a powerfully enslaving sin, then He is able to rescue you as well.

Make whatever call you need to make.

Finish it.

Don't just *pray* the prayer of Jabez; *live* the victory we have in Jesus.

PART V

NEW HORIZONS
WITH GOD

And Jabez called on the God of Israel saying,
"Oh, that You would bless me indeed,
and enlarge my territory,
that Your hand would be with me,
and that You would keep me from evil,
that I may not cause pain!"
So God granted him what he requested.

COSTLY INVESTMENT, INFINITE RETURN

Well done, Ordinary! the Dream Giver said.
You are a good and faithful Dreamer. Now let me show you more.
"More?" asked Ordinary. *More,* said the Dream Giver.
There's so much more of my Big Dream waiting for you.[1]

T H E   D R E A M   G I V E R

*I*saiah was sure he would die.

In his vision he stood in the very temple of God in heaven. The Holy One Himself was seated on His throne, high and lifted up, His majesty and glory outshining the brightest sun. Around Him flew seraphim—among the most awesome beings in creation—who cried out, "Holy, holy, holy!" in voices that caused the ground to quake.

The terrified Isaiah felt the impact of his sinfulness in the presence of Perfection personified.

"Woe is me!" he cried out. "I'm a dead man! For I am full

of sin and my eyes have seen the King, the Lord of Hosts!"

But one of the seraphim took a live coal from the altar and flew to Isaiah. He touched Isaiah's mouth with the coal, purging his sin, purifying him before Holy God. He was clean!

That's when the Lord Almighty called from His throne, "Whom shall I send? Who will go for Us?"

In an instant, Isaiah comprehended the situation. Throughout his life he had dreamed of serving his God in some significant way. Here in the awesome Presence, he had no doubt that power was available for anything God wanted to do. And the freshly cleansed Isaiah knew that evil would no longer hinder God's working in his life.

The God of the universe was asking for a volunteer. It was the chance of a lifetime.

"Me!" Isaiah cried. "Here I am! Send me!"

And God did (see Isaiah 6:1–10).

YOU'RE THE ONE

The Lord is still looking for volunteers.

He wants ordinary people who trust the goodness of His giving heart. People who will ask for the blessings He longs to pour out.

He wants men and women who know they are nobodies but who beg Him, *Lord, let me do more for You!* Men and women who will serve Him faithfully as He expands their borders.

He wants servants who know their own limitations. Who daily cast themselves into His mighty hand, that He might achieve through them dreams that they could never achieve by themselves.

He wants hearts of contrition, pleading, *Remove my darkness! Keep me from evil, that my service be not hindered!*

God is calling to you.

Your answer starts with a single, small step.

I know, it feels like a big step.

But swallow hard, push through the invisible wall of fear, and answer, "Send me!"

Don't wait for an emotion. Make a decision.

You'll be choosing a new way to live. Yes, you will feel fear. And there will be a price. But if you give God your life, you'll bask in the infinite pleasure of His "Well done!" throughout all eternity.

What's more, your life on earth will never be dull. Start praying with the heart of Jabez. There's nothing magic about his words, but there is something special about the honorable character they represent. Commit to praying fervently day after day until God shows up.

And He will. Why? Because you'll be praying His will. He *wants* to bless you. He *wants* to enlarge your borders. He *wants* to unleash His power on your behalf. He *wants* to keep you from evil.

You don't have to convince Him.

A New You for a New Life

Every human being on earth—whether he admits it or not—carries in his soul a dream, a sense of destiny, a longing for something greater than himself. God is the Dream Giver, and only He can fulfill your deepest desire.

You might respond sadly, "I want to do something great

for God, but somewhere along the way, my big dream crumbled to dust."

Leave the past in the past! Paul did. He stopped lamenting what was behind, because he couldn't fix it. And he fastened his gaze firmly on the goal that God placed in front of him. He gave up everything he had, counting it worthless, because *it was worthless* in comparison to gaining Jesus Christ and the abundant life (see Philippians 3:7–14).

Your answer starts with a single, small step.

Do this and you'll embark on an unimaginable adventure.

Over the months and years, you will change. You will grow to trust God's promises and recognize His truth. You'll become more holy in character. You'll learn to stand your ground and fight with God's hand upon you.

You'll discover that the values you used to hold are not as important anymore, and you'll begin wanting what God wants. As you give up the life you thought you needed, you'll find yourself getting more of God Himself. And He will so satisfy your heart that all other passions will be consumed in your longing for Him.

The further you walk with Him, the more He will ask of you. More of your money, more of your service, more of your time. He'll even ask you to give Him your big dream.

Until all that's left is one person—Jesus Christ. One day you'll awaken to the fact that you've chosen Him as your supreme purpose in life, and you'll realize that He Himself has been your greatest dream, your longing, your desperate desire all along.

This will cost you everything. But the return is infinite.

Hand over your life and you'll receive *abundant* life, which you can enjoy here and now and throughout all eternity.

The beginning of true fulfillment will come as you pray, "Lord, use me. Please send me someone who needs You. Or send me where I can serve." And soon you will see His answer. You will touch a life or advance an eternal cause. You'll see fruit of lasting value accumulate and multiply before your eyes.

And if you've ever wondered if your life was significant or whether you would ever make a difference, these questions will never cross your mind again. Your life will be pleasing to you as you know that your life is pleasing to God.

It's what you were made for!

NOTES

Introduction

1. *The Prayer of Jabez*, Bruce Wilkinson (Sisters, OR: Multnomah Publishers, 2000), 24.

Chapter 1

1. *The Dream Giver*, Bruce Wilkinson (Sisters, OR: Multnomah Publishers, 2003), 13–14.
2. "Pay It Godward" by Denny and Leesa Bellesi.
3. "Never Too Late" by JoAn Cutler.

Chapter 2

1. *The Prayer of Jabez*, 17.
2. "The Heavens Declare His Glory" by Judy Salisbury.
3. "God Granted Her Request" by Christine Thompson.
4. "God Will Provide" by Anne Austin and children.

Chapter 3

1. "Blind Faith" by Patsy Elsea.
2. "A Fish Story" by James Quillman, as told to Alesia Campbell.

Chapter 4

1. *The Prayer of Jabez*, 24.
2. "Expanding the Borders of the Heart" by Carol Milhouse.

Chapter 5

1. *The Dream Giver,* 21.
2. "The Song of Jabez" by John Waller.
3. *The Dream Giver,* 93.

Chapter 6

1. *The Dream Giver,* 70–71.
2. "Prayer o' the Irish" by Michael Conners.

Chapter 7

1. *The Prayer of Jabez Devotional,* Bruce Wilkinson (Sisters, OR: Multnomah Publishers, 2001), 56.
2. "Blessings Behind Prison Walls" by Ryan Minesinger.
3. "Who Wants to Be a Believer?" by Burton Villaverde.

Chapter 8

1. *The Dream Giver,* 145.

Chapter 10

1. *The Dream Giver,* 145.
2. "Along the Jabez Journey" by Barbara Baumgardner.
3. "Limits That Release" by Deana Butler.

Chapter 11

1. *The Prayer of Jabez,* 65.

Chapter 13

1. *The Prayer of Jabez*, 69.
2. "The Decision" by Steve Hershberger.
3. "Set Free, Indeed" by Virginia Howell.

Chapter 14

1. *The Dream Giver*, 65.

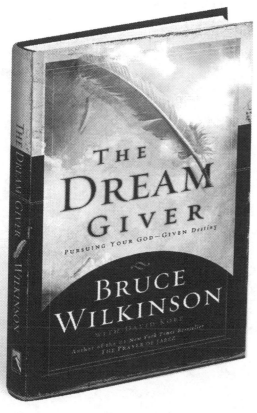

THE DREAM GIVER SERIES

The Dream Giver for Teens

It's time to begin the journey of a lifetime! Let Bruce and Jessica Wilkinson help you find your dream and pursue it on a quest to discover the life you've always dreamed of.

ISBN 1-59052-459-4

The Dream Giver for Couples

Let Bruce and Darlene Marie Wilkinson take you on a journey that will give you hope as you discover the seven principles to experiencing the marriage you've always dreamed of.

ISBN 1-59052-460-8

The Dream Giver for Parents

In this practical guide, Bruce and Darlene Marie Wilkinson share with you the seven secrets for guiding your children to discover and pursue their dreams.

ISBN 1-59052-455-1

The Dream Giver
DVD & VHS

Live your dream. That is the key message from #1 *New York Times* bestselling author Bruce Wilkinson. This visual adaptation of the bestselling book invites you to follow your heart and find your destiny in an inspired life dream that is uniquely yours. Taking up where *The Prayer of Jabez* left off, this will show you how to "expand your borders" for your greatest fulfillment and for the great honor of the Dream Giver.

DVD UPC 01871381 6788

VHS UPC 01871343 4081

DVD Special Features

Appearances by:
- Rick Warren (author of *A Purpose Driven Life*)
- Kirk Cameron (Left Behind series) • George Foreman
- Kirk Franklin • John Tesh • And many more!

The BreakThrough Series

ISBN 1-57673-733-0

ISBN 1-57673-975-9

ISBN 1-57673-976-7

"Fastest selling book of all time."
—*Publishers Weekly*

The Prayer of Jabez

Are you ready to reach for the extraordinary? To ask God for the abundant blessings He longs to give you? Join Bruce Wilkinson to discover how the remarkable prayer of a little-known Bible hero can release God's favor, power, and protection. You'll see how one daily prayer can help you leave the past behind...and break through to the life you were meant to live!

Secrets of the Vine

Dr. Bruce Wilkinson explores John 15 to show readers how to make maximum impact for God. Dr. Wilkinson demonstrates how Jesus is the Vine of life, discusses four levels of "fruit bearing" (doing the good work of God), and reveals three life-changing truths that will lead readers to new joy and effectiveness in His kingdom.

A Life God Rewards

Bruce Wilkinson, author of the #1 *New York Times* bestseller *The Prayer of Jabez*, shows why it's worth it—at a thousand percent return on investment—to serve God with all your heart for all your life!

GOING DEEPER WITH JABEZ

The Prayer of Jabez Teaching Series
An 8-part curriculum from Bruce Wilkinson

Dear Friend,
The adventure before you is one more chapter in a spiritual phenomenon. Jabez's prayer continues to spark quiet revolutions in the lives of ordinary people like you and me. Has it happened in your life yet? *⸶* I hope so. But even if you've already set out on the Jabez journey, this video course will take you deeper into the prayer, wider into the blessings and further than ever into expanding your ministry for God.

Bruce I Wilkinson

Available in DVD and VHS.
Great for personal or group study!

DVD 19.95 SRP 0766219291
VHS 14.95 SRP 0766219283

DVD

Also available in audio CD and Cassettes.
Ideal for drive-time listening!

CD   19.99 SRP 0972007490
Cassette 19.99 SRP 0972007458

Workbook and Leader's Guide available.
Perfect for group study.

Workbook 5.99 SRP 1576739392
Leader's Guide 4.99 SRP 1576739384

For more information, call **866-263-7822**,
or visit **www.brucewilkinson.com**
Visit your local retailer to find these products.

Global Vision
RESOURCES™

Expand your territory.
Come to Africa . . .
come change the world.
The Good News: You can make a difference!

Hunger:
Never Ending Gardens

Orphans:
African Dream Villages

Poverty:
Mega Farms

Aids:
Beat the Drum

Dream for Africa (DFA) is a faith-based humanitarian movement that mobilizes volunteers to address the critical problems of hunger, orphans, poverty and AIDS in Africa. DFA seeks to recruit 10,000 volunteers next year.

4 reasons to help:

1 200 million Africans are undernourished

2 Death and disease create 10,000 orphans every week

3 Most Africans live on less than $1 per day

4 70% of the World's HIV/AIDS population is in Africa

Come to Africa or become a Dream Giver.

For more information visit
www.dreamforafrica.com

DREAM for AFRICA
Hunger · Orphans · Poverty · AIDS

Printed in the United States
by Baker & Taylor Publisher Services